HELPING YOUR CHILD ACHIEVE IN SCHOOL

—*Strategies for Caring Parents*—

Erratum

Pages 124 and 125 have been transposed with pages 126 and 127. Please accept our apologies.

HELPING YOUR CHILD ACHIEVE IN SCHOOL

—— Strategies for Caring Parents ——

by
Dr. Barbara Johnson

Arena Press
Novato, California

Editor: Betty Lou Kratoville
Art: Masters Agency
Typesetting: Pamela Nye
Paste-up: Bill Moore
Jeanette Wendt

This book was set in English Times and printed at Braun-Brumfield, Ann Arbor, Michigan.

FIRST EDITION

Library of Congress Cataloging in Publication Data

Johnson, Barbara, 1950-
    Helping your child achieve in school.

    1. Reading (Elementary)   2. Home and school.
3. Learning ability.   I. Title.
LB1573.J543   1985   372.4   84-28417
ISBN 0-87879-465-4

85 86 87 88 89 10 9 8 7 6 5 4 3 2 1

ACKNOWLEDGEMENTS

As with the writing of any book, there are many people to thank . . .

- Dr. Lynn McCarthy for continual encouragement and her contributions to several chapters
- Patricia Walsh for challenging and questioning my ideas
- My editor, Betty Lou Kratoville, for her knowledge and advice
- My husband, Edward, for his constant encouragement through the ups and downs of writing the book
- Irmgard Barnes for countless hours spent in typing
- Ann Lee Dugan for the tedious business of proofreading
- My mother and father, Raymond and Winona Wiese, whose guidance helped me reach my potential. My highest hope is that all parents provide their children with such "gifts."

. . . Barbara E. Johnson

TABLE OF CONTENTS

The little world of childhood with its familiar surroundings is a model of the greater world. The more intensively the family has stamped its character upon the child, the more it will tend to feel and see its earlier miniature world again in the bigger world of adult life.

. . . *From* Psychological Reflections:
A Jung Anthology

INTRODUCTION

What do you want most for your child? Good health? Of course! What else? A good education may well be the next item on your list of priorities. But there is much more to it than that. Education should be exhilarating and exciting, not drudgery. Education should expand your child's curiosity about his world, not stamp it out. Education should be a springboard for his potential, not a deep pit of failure and frustration. As a parent, you want to be sure your child's educational experience is rich and rewarding and successful. Yet, as a parent, you may not always know what you can do to ensure a good start, to lend a hand over the inevitable hurdles, and to serve as a constant source of support and reinforcement. That's why this book has been written. That's why you have it in your possession.

But a word of caution . . . Have you ever gone to a restaurant and been served so much food you didn't know where to start? In a sense, this book is like that — it's an enormous "banquet" of suggestions and ideas. No parent, no matter how dedicated, could be expected to digest it all. The matter of choice — which idea best fits the child's

1

needs—is up to the parent, who, after all, knows the child better than anyone else. The important point here is that no parent should feel guilty for a single moment because all suggestions cannot be used. Just select from the "menu" offered—and enjoy!

It must be mentioned in the light of current philosophy that personal pronouns are one of the most tedious problems with which an author must cope. We are well aware that children come in two packages—"he's" and "she's"—as do teachers. In an attempt at fairness and clarity, in this book all children will be referred to as "he's" and all teachers as "she's." There may be a better way to solve this problem, but we've not discovered it.

Because you have this book in your possession, we know that you are dedicated to helping your child achieve in school. There may be times when you grow weary of the task you have set yourself, and that's quite all right! You are human, too, and have a perfect right to be discouraged and disheartened. Just as you are not expected to follow every suggestion set forth, no one is implying that you must work with your child 365 days a year—so take time out, and you'll return to the task refreshed and renewed. Best of all, we're convinced you will find that you are a better "teacher" than you ever dreamed. Good luck!

Chapter 1

THE CHILD'S FIRST TEACHER

As a parent, of course you are interested in your child's receiving a good education. Naturally, you want to provide your child with every opportunity to learn, to enjoy learning about new things, and to continue his curiosity about the world in which he lives. But, as a parent, you may not always know what to provide for your child so he can achieve his own potential.

The parents, in the following stories, experience difficulties in knowing the right things to do for their children. In each situation, the parents want the best for their son or daughter. They are willing to do almost anything. As you read, you may recognize some similarities between these children and your own. You may find you've asked some of the same questions or have had some of the same feelings.

• Today is the end of the semester. Jim has been dreading it for a long time. The bell rings. Jim's teacher hands out the sixth-grade report cards. Jim won't look at his since it says the same old thing—an F in reading, D in English. Jim knows his parents

3

will be disappointed so he decides to hide his report card. Instead of making his typical grand entrance, Jim slips into the house, hiding his report card underneath his coat. He lurks up to his room, safely burying the report card underneath his clothes in the bottom drawer. Two weeks later, his mother is putting clean clothes away and discovers the report card and poor grades. At first, she is angry. But gradually her anger changes to understanding and sadness. She knows Jim has tried hard to improve, but his effort doesn't seem to change his grades. She is frustrated and wonders what she can do to help her son learn to read.

• Juliann White has just finished first grade and cannot read. She is about the only one who hasn't finished the first reading book. The Whites wonder if there is something wrong with Juliann. Is she a slow learner? Should Juliann repeat first grade? Should she be tested for learning disabilities? Perhaps there is a problem with the teacher or the reading program used in Juliann's school. The Whites are confused and want advice from other educational experts. Where can they receive unbiased information?

• The Jacobsons are concerned about their son's reading habits. Mark Jacobson is in junior high and receives good grades in school. However, he seldom reads for enjoyment. Most of his free time is spent in sports activities as well as playing video games. The Jacobsons cannot understand why Mark doesn't enjoy reading books like *Call of the Wild, Huckleberry Finn, David Copperfield,* et cetera. When they were his age, they both were avid readers. And even today, both Jacobsons regularly read newspapers, magazines, and books. Mark has plenty of his own books and his own library card. The Jacobsons wonder, "What else can parents do to instill a love for reading?"

• Four-year-old Lisa wants to learn to read. She wants to hear the same story over and over. If her mother changes a word, Lisa chimes, "That's not right, Mommy." Lisa loves to copy words and asks how to spell some of her favorite words. If her mother doesn't respond immediately, Lisa makes up the spelling. Surprisingly, Lisa's messages are easily read! The other day she wrote this message: "I wet to the zoo and I wet to mi gramo and I wet to see the fom." Lisa often sits with a book, turning the pages and reciting the story by heart. Lisa's parents wonder if they should encourage and help their child learn to read. If she learns to read, will she be bored in school? And what if they teach her incorrectly—will this harm her?

Are any of these situations familiar? Or are you concerned that one of these experiences could be yours in the near future? In this book, I hope to provide you with information and guidance to answer your questions, cope with possible reading problems, and provide help in solving them. Throughout the book, I'll suggest simple and enjoyable activities to help develop your child's reading skills. I'll also discuss what the schools are doing to help your child's reading achievement. We will also explore how you and the teacher can work together to increase your child's reading ability.

Parents are *vital* to their child's educational development. Research studies show that parents can be a positive influence on their child's learning. If you surround your child with interesting toys and games, and share a variety of experiences, you can improve his ability to learn. And if you always try to answer your child's questions, learning will grow naturally. When you display confidence in your child, he feels secure. And when you show your approval as he learns new things, he, too, will take delight in learning.

To take a positive and active role in your child's learning to read, let's first look at how children learn.

5

What is Learning?

Learning is the process of taking in and remembering information we need. We use our senses primarily to take in information about the outside world. Drawing a picture from memory, playing a piece of music by ear, finding one's way through a dark room by touch are a few examples of how we use our senses to learn. And the way we take in information affects how it is remembered. When teachers speak of three methods of learning—visual (sight), auditory (hearing), and kinesthetic (touch)—they are talking about the three senses we use to learn. As adults, we use all three senses, usually in combination, but it was as children that we learned how to use our senses effectively. Let's consider each sense separately. We'll look first at how children use their eyes to learn.

Seeing and Learning

Most of our world is geared toward visual experiences. Flashing lights, bright colors, enormous signs, and, of course, television, give us information through our eyes. This information is then stored in our brain. However, we do not all use the same method for remembering. We tend to assume that others see things the same way we see them, but people use different ways to remember visual information. Take a look at how *you* remember things you've seen by answering the following questions:

1. Picture the room where you sleep. Do you "see" it in color or black and white? (Not everyone remembers visual colors.)
   a. Now move all the furniture in the room. Put the bed under the window; move a chest of drawers next to the closet. Is this *easy* or *hard* for you to do?
   b. Try to paint the room yellow. Put sheer curtains on the windows. Now paint red polka dots on the walls. Can you see the

redecorated room in your mind? There are many adults who would not be able to see this new room.

Do you depend on your sense of sight to remember information? Think about this as you answer the next two questions.

2. When you walk into a house, can you redecorate it in your mind, including rearranged walls, new colors, and your own furniture in place?

3. When you're on a trip, try studying a map of a new town. Can you then take a friend on a tour of the town? Many adults can read a two-dimensional map and then transfer that information to a real town. This person is able to take in information in one way and use it in a new situation.

Hearing and Learning

Information is not only seen, but heard as well. Some people can learn incredible amounts of information just from listening. Their sense of hearing is a valuable tool for learning. The story of the great composer, Beethoven, illustrates our keen ability to use hearing for remembering and creating. Beethoven was unaware of his hearing loss because of his strong memory for hearing a previous sound. If Beethoven saw a book fall, he was able to remember the "sound" of the book hitting the floor even though he was almost totally deaf. Playwrights are often credited with having a keen sense for hearing dialogue and committing it to memory. Many claim that while writing a play they are able to "hear" their characters speak. Composers are also able to "hear" the melody of the song even though it's only on paper. Musicians often use the record "Orchestra Minus One." This is a recorded symphony with all but one of the instruments playing. Most musicians are able to play the missing instrument in their minds.

Adults are able to keep a large number of songs in their memories. Often a song can be identified after hearing only three notes. Do you rely on your sense of hearing to learn information? Answer the following questions to find out.

1. Remember the last time you read a play. When reading the dialogue, were you able to "hear" the characters talking? Some adults "hear" female voices, male voices, and even the shouts of throngs of people.

2. When you studied for a test in a history course, did you read your notes out loud? When it was necessary to remember the three causes of World War I, did you "hear" yourself listing the three reasons?

3. When you meet a person with a complicated name in a noisy room, are you able to remember the name when you hear it? If so, you are relying on hearing for learning information.

Touching and Learning

From cradle on, youngsters seem to learn through touch. What babies have not placed every new object in their mouths! As an adult, you may find that writing everything down is necessary for remembering because recall is simplified through the use of touch in writing. This learning method of using touch is called the kinesthetic method. Tennis and golf instructors often emphasize the feel of a basic swing or movement. (This method may also combine the sense of hearing with the sense of touch. The player may also be encouraged to listen to the sound of the ball hitting the racquet in a successful shot and then try to duplicate that sound with the same body movement.) Many skiers and golfers can sit down after a downhill run or game and re-experience the entire event through the body movement.

Many stories have been told of prisoners of war who have spent long hours in solitary confinement and still emerged in good mental health. One fascinating story from the Korean War tells of a prisoner who "played golf" every day of his three-year confinement. He came from a small town and knew every part of the local golf course. When he returned home, his game had actually improved even though he had been kept in a four-foot square room for three years.

Test yourself! Do you readily use the sense of touch to learn?

1. When you have to study for a test, do you have to rewrite all your notes? Can you remember writing the notes? Can you feel the notes being written? Can you see in your mind your written notes?

2. When you meet a person with a complicated name, do you have to write his name down to remember it?

3. When you finish a dance, sport, or exercise of any kind, can you relive the feelings of the exercise? Do you feel your muscles move while sitting down? If so, you are learning through touch.

Combining the Senses for Learning

The brain is able to use all three senses together for learning. If your child is able to use these three learning methods, he fits the mold of educational learning in this country. The child who is unable to learn through these three senses is often at high risk for school failure. The incompatibility of this child's learning and the school's teaching is at odds. Or this same child may be identified as learning disabled, reading disabled, or a slow learner.

Learning to read requires the child to use all three senses: sight, hearing, and touch. Teachers use reading methods based on one, two, or all three of the senses. Before specific reading methods are discussed, let's consider what reading is all about.

What Is Reading?

Before reading beyond this sentence, try to define reading. Compare your definition to this one:

- Reading is *understanding* words and ideas.
- Reading is communication. The author is sending a message to the reader.
- Reading involves thinking, analyzing, and applying acquired knowledge. A reader's prior understanding of the world affects the meaning acquired from a passage.

Think about this definition of reading as you read the next paragraph.

With hocked gems financing him, our hero bravely defied all scornful laughter that tried to prevent his scheme. "Your eyes deceive," he had said. "An egg, not a table, correctly typifies this unexplored planet." Now three sturdy sisters sought proof. Forging along, sometimes through calm vastness, yet more often over turbulent peaks and valleys, days became weeks as many doubters spread fearful rumors about the edge. At last, from nowhere welcome winged creatures appeared signifying momentous success.

("Effects of Comprehension on Prose," by D.J. Dooling and R. Lachman, *Journal of Experimental Psychology, 1971.*)

Could you read this paragraph? Did you understand the author's message? Were you able to think through, analyze, and understand the author's ideas? Probably not—reading requires more than "saying the words." Now reread the paragraph knowing the paragraph is about Christopher Columbus.

Wasn't the paragraph easier to understand? As soon as the topic was known, the information you knew about Christopher Columbus was easily remembered and connected to the paragraph. Now you were able to think about what the author was saying and his message was easily communicated to you, the reader.

It is the exchange of ideas between the author and the reader that gives meaning to reading. The heart of reading is understanding the author's message. If your child is not understanding the passage, he isn't reading.

But how does your child begin to read and develop into a good reader? Well, we know the beginning reader is quite different from the skilled reader. Let's look at how these two readers differ.

Beginning and Skilled Readers: The Difference

The beginning reader reads every word on the page and gives each word equal importance. However, the skilled reader reads only those words that are necessary to understand the author's message. The skilled reader knows which words are important to understand. Previous experiences and knowledge about language indicate which words are important and which are not and help to make accurate predictions about words and meaning. For the skilled reader, individual words are not as important as knowing information about the topic and using acquired language ability to understand the author's ideas.

Let's look a little further into the skilled reader's expertise. Why does he rely so much on language knowledge and experiences? Among other things, the skilled reader has a highly-developed understanding of how language works. He knows which one of these groups of words is a sentence:

1. The children
2. The children laughed at the clown.

He also knows that words in a sentence have a logical order so the sentence makes sense. A skilled reader would laugh if he read this sentence:

The floor bounced on the ball.

It's not necessary for the skilled reader to define each word in a sentence because he looks at the relationships among the words to understand writing. His knowledge of what a sentence is helps him to read. Because he knows what a sentence should look like, he can predict, then be assured that what he reads makes sense. Because you are a skilled reader, you'll easily read the following message:

Carol went shopping and saw a coat in the ___1___. She thought the coat was a beautiful one and she ___2___ her mother over to see it. Carol's mother saw ___3___ coat and ___4___ thought it was pretty, too. Carol was ___5___ that her mother liked this coat. Carol then decided to buy it.

Did you notice how your knowledge of language helped you predict the right words for the blanks? These are the exact responses: (1) window, (2) called, (3) the, (4) she, and (5) happy. How many of your responses were similar to the "exact" responses? Your knowledge of how language works is not found on the printed page but in your mind.

The skilled reader has another advantage over the beginning reader: a knowledge and effortless use of the sound and letter relationships of the English language. Schools refer to sound and letter relationship as *phonics*. The skilled reader automatically associates a sound with the alphabet letter. Most of the time the association is correct, but sometimes it's not because the English language doesn't always have a perfect match between sound and letter. As you know, sometimes the letter "o" has the sound as in "cool," and sometimes it has the sound as in "coat." Or it has a dozen other sounds. How does the skilled reader figure this out? By reading frequently, the skilled reader has learned to use both sentence meaning and the sounds of language to recognize words.

Language is only one ability that separates the skilled reader from the beginner. Unlike a beginner, the skilled reader has vast experiences and broad knowledge to help him understand the author's ideas. Think for a moment about your ability to read a novel or an article about something you know. How fast can you read familiar material and understand it, too? Do you seem to read every word on the page, or do your eyes skip over words? Most likely your answer is, "I read the material quickly, but don't read every word."

To become a skilled reader, the beginner must learn to use both language and experiences while reading. The activities in this book are aimed at helping our beginners do just that!

The Beginning Reader

The beginning reader knows how to speak and can draw on experiences. However, in most cases, the beginning reader has not made the connection between the knowledge in his head and the information in the book. The beginning reader has not developed an understanding of how oral language relates to written language.

Whereas the skilled reader reads fluently, the beginner tends to read in a slow, halting fashion which hinders his comprehension. Is slow reading due to slow eye movements? Does the beginner need eye movement training? No! Some children have faulty eye movements, but this is usually due to a physical problem requiring an eye specialist. For the most part, beginning readers have the same number of pauses in their reading as the skilled reader. The difference between the beginning and the skilled reader is not what the eye does but what the brain is able to understand. It is the brain that controls the eye. The brain tells the eye where to focus so that the brain can understand the passage. Then the brain interprets the author's message so the reader can make predictions while reading. As the brain makes sense of the text, it continually selects future places to pause so it can build comprehension. Once the beginning reader can apply his knowledge of language and develop a wide variety of experiences, he, too, will turn into a skilled reader, just as the caterpillar gradually changes into a beautiful butterfly.

13

Try to read the following material.

+⊓⊗ (Are) 2≠⌐ (you) ⊥∪0⊐ (sick)?
+⊓⊗ 2≠⌐ ⌐◇+∪∧∪8∩ (waiting) ∇≠⊓ (for) ∧0⊗ (the)
∐≠0∧≠⊓ (doctor)?

◇⊗ (We) +⊓⊗ 8≠∧ (not) ⊥∪0⊐.
◇⊗ +⊓⊗ ◇+∪∧∪8∩ ∇≠⊓ ≠⌐⊓ (our) ?≠∧0⊗⊓ (mother).

+⊓⊗ 2≠⌐ ⊥∪0⊐?
+⊓⊗ 2≠⌐ ◇+∪∧∪8∩ ∇≠⊓ ∧0⊗ ∐≠0∧≠⊓?

∪(I) +?(am) ⊥∪0⊐.
∪ +? ◇+∪∧∪8∩ ∇≠⊓ ∧0⊗ ∐≠0∧≠⊓.
∪⊥(Is) 2≠⌐⊓(your) ?≠∧0⊗⊓ ⊥∪0⊐?

(Paul McKee: *Primer for Parents,* Copyright ©1975 Houghton Mifflin Company. Used with permission.)

14

Was it easy to read? Notice how your reading was slowed down or even halted. What caused this? One reason could be that you didn't know the sound-letter relationships used in this material. It should be no surprise then that the beginning reader has an experience with written English similar to the one you had with this material.

Suggestions for Parents

1. Read to your child. No matter what age your child happens to be, he will benefit from listening to you read aloud. The books you choose should contain all types of fiction: folk tales, fantasy, realistic fiction, mysteries. When you select books, take a look at different authors and the way they get a reader interested. For example, read a novel containing satire, and help your child become aware of the author's purpose for using satire. Your child will not only learn various types of literature, but may also see reading as enjoyable. Reading aloud also may motivate your child to read other books. If he is presently a non-reader, it may give him the desire to learn to read. To help you select books, study *Choosing Books for Children: A Commonsense Guide* by Betsy Hearne.

2. Discuss the books you read to your child. Simple discussions about favorite characters, enjoyable events, new ideas, and just "what happened" will help your child understand the importance and enjoyment of reading.

3. Introduce your child to books that discuss his hobby, interests, or new experiences. Factual books can develop a whole new world for your child. New horizons can be opened or expanded. After your child reads a book about his hobby, interest, or new experience, discuss with him what he already knows and what he learned that

15

was new, the same, or different. These discussions should help your child combine his knowledge with that of the author. You'll soon notice how his comprehension improves.

4. Provide many varied experiences for your child. The more first-hand experiences your child has, the more knowledge he can bring to reading. Going to museums, arboretums, forest preserves, and community events will expand his knowledge, his learning, and his reading.

5. Listen and talk to your child. Try to avoid the pitfalls of talking at a level of baby talk, simple vocabulary, and simple sentence structure. Children can understand and should be exposed to a vast number of words and complex sentences. You will be surprised how their vocabulary and their ability to use a wide variety of sentences will increase. Speaking "down to children" or using "baby talk" will only limit your child's language growth.

6. Subscribe to children's magazines so your child has reading material geared to his age and interest level. Invite him to choose one or more of the magazines. Here is a list of some current publications for children. For more information, you may want to consult *Guide to Children's Magazines, Newspapers, Reference Books* prepared by Judy Matthews and Lillian Drag. (Association for Childhood International, 1974.)

Ages 2—5

Children's Playmate
1100 Waterway Blvd.
Box 567B
Indianapolis, IN 46206

Highlights for Children
P.O. Box 269
Columbus, OH 43216

Humpty Dumpty's Magazine
Parent's Magazine Enterprises, Inc.
52 Vanderbilt Ave.
New York, NY 10017

Sesame Street Magazine
P.O. Box 2896
Boulder, CO 80302

Your Big Backyard
National Wildlife Federation
1412 6th Street, NW
Washington D.C. 20036

Ages 6—8

Boy's Life
P.O. Box 6130
Dallas/Fort Worth Airport, TX 75261

Cricket
Box 2671
Boulder, CO 80302

Children's Playmate
1100 Waterway Blvd.
Box 567B
Indianapolis, IN 46206

Daisy
Daisy Subscription Service
P.O. Box 2466
Boulder, CO 80302

Electric Company Magazine
200 Watt Street
P.O. Box 925
Boulder, CO 80302

Ebony Jr!
Johnson Publishing Co.
820 S. Michigan
Chicago, IL 60605

Highlights for Children
P.O. Box 269
Columbus, OH 43216

Humpty Dumpty's Magazine
Parent's Magazine Enterprises, Inc.
52 Vanderbilt Ave.
New York, NY 10017

Jack and Jill
1100 Waterway Blvd.
Box 567B
Indianapolis, IN 46206

National Geographic World
Dept. 00683
17th and M St. NW
Washington D.C. 20036

Ranger Rick's Nature Magazine
8925 Leesburg Pike
Vienna, VA 22180

Ages 9−12

Boy's Life
P.O. Box 6130
Dallas/Fort Worth Airport, TX 75261

Child's Life
Benjamin Franklin Literary
and Medical Society, Inc.
Youth Publications
1100 Waterway Blvd.
Box 567B
Indianapolis, IN 46206

Cobblestone (history)
Box 959
Farmingdale, NY 11737

Crafts 'n Things
14 Main St.
Park Ridge, IL 60068

Daisy
Daisy Subscription Service
P.O. Box 2466
Boulder, CO 80302

Dynamite
654 Count Morbida's Castle
Marion, OH 43302

Ebony Jr!
Johnson Publishing Co.
820 S. Michigan
Chicago, IL 60605

Highlights for Children
P.O. Box 269
Columbus, OH 43216

Jack and Jill
1100 Waterway Blvd.
Box 567B
Indianapolis, IN 46206

National Geographic World
Dept. 00683
17th and M St. NW
Washington D.C. 20036

Odyssey
Astro Media Corp.
P.O. Box 92788
Milwaukee, WI 53202

Ranger Rick's Nature Magazine
8925 Leesburg Pike
Vienna, VA 22180

Science Land
501 Fifth Ave.
New York, NY 10017

3-2-1 Contact
Children's Television Workshop
One Lincoln Plaza
New York, NY 10023

7. Be a good reading "model" by letting your child see you read. If you read daily, your child can see a need for learning to read. Children understand and imitate family attitudes toward reading.

8. Create an environment that encourages your child to read. An inviting chair, a cozy corner, a soft, over-sized pillow will make an appealing place to read.

9. Buy books as presents for your child, and he'll learn to value books.

10. Make sure your child has a library card. Start taking him to the library as a very young child. Help him to select the books you'll be reading aloud. The library habit should begin as soon as he is old enough to understand the rules for quiet behavior.

"It's not that I'm a slow learner — I'm just a **fast forgetter!**"

Chapter 2

HOW READING BEGINS

"Want to hear me read?" asked three-year-old Tracey as she confidently took out the book, *Madeline*. Seriously looking at the first page, she began:

> In an old house in Paris that is covered with vines,
> Lived twelve little girls in two straight lines.
> In two straight lines they broke their bread,
> and brushed their teeth and went to bed.
>
> (From MADELINE by Ludwig Bemelmans. Copyright ©1939 by Ludwig Bemelmans. Copyright renewed ©1967 by Madeline Bemelmans and Barbara Bemelmans Marciano. Reprinted by permission of Viking Penguin Inc.)

She read right to the last page. With pride, Tracey closed the book as the adults in the room oohed and ahhed over this impressive performance. Equally impressed with the stir she had caused, Tracey decided to outdo her accomplishment. "That's nothing! Watch me read with my eyes closed." And she began to recite: "In an old house in Paris . . . " right to the last page. Tracey had every adult in the room believing that she was reading. Her expression and the turning of each page at the right moment showed that this young child knew what reading should be. She was expertly modeling the basic concept of reading: reading is communication. She was "pre-reading."

The first step in learning to read is to realize that the black marks on the page represent another form of communication—the written form. The next step is to figure out what those black marks stand for. Eventually, the young reader learns to recognize words quickly and readily and to use information learned from books. But these skills don't develop overnight! They are learned over time with regular practice.

Reading Readiness

How does a child learn to be a skilled reader? Not an easy question to answer! The pre-reader is at a stage referred to as "reading readiness." This means that specific skills need to be acquired before a child can easily learn to read: oral language, vision, hearing, and direction. Interest in learning to read as well as rich and varied experiences also benefit the beginning reader.

Oral Language

Oral language is an important part of reading. Speech provides the child with the basic concepts of language: sounds, grammar, and meanings. The child can use knowledge of oral language as a reference for reading. Learning to read is much easier for the child who can rely on oral language to make sense out of print. If the child has a poor command of sentence structure, a small vocabulary, and poor pronunciation, he may find reading a difficult task.

As a parent, you may find it helpful to know how your child's oral language skills compare to other children his age. If his oral language skills are following a normal growth pattern, these skills should help him with reading. In the following chart, you will find the average language abilities of a child during a specific stage of development. These averages are based on research in the field of language development and were drawn from the work of E.H. Lennenberg; R.J. Smith and D.D. Johnson; M.C. Templin; B. Wood.

Developmental Stages in Children's Language

(Ages 4 months to 6 years)

4 Months	Coos and chuckles
6–9 Months	Babbles continually (e.g., gagaga, dadada)
12–18 Months	Uses small number of words, understands easy commands, imitates sounds
18–21 Months	Uses 20–200 words, understands simple questions, forms two- to three-word sentences
24–27 Months	Uses 300–400 words, talks in short sentences containing prepositions and pronouns, talks often with poor rhythm and fluency
30–33 Months	Has made great increases in size of vocabulary, uses three-to four-word sentences that sound adultlike
36–39 Months	Uses 1,000 words or more, talks in well-formed sentences, 80 percent follow grammatical rules, can be understood by others
48–60 Months or 4-5 Years	Talks extensively as he does activities, asks many questions such as "Why," can identify by name the objects found in picture books and magazines, can follow simple commands even if objects are not in sight, repeats words continuously such as syllables, phrases, and sounds
60–72 Months or 5-6 Years	Can readily use descriptive words (adjectives and adverbs), can use simple opposites such as big and little, small and large, can be completely understood even though pronunciation is not precise, can repeat nine word sentences, can define everyday objects by how they are used, can follow three sequential commands

Don't be alarmed if your child's language skills vary slightly. However, if there are great discrepancies, you should seek professional advice from your pediatrician or a speech and language clinic. In many states, a law requires local school districts to provide speech screening and training for children ages 4-21. The school district can then conduct the necessary tests to identify whether or not your child has a language problem.

It is common for a child of three to drop the "l" or "r" sound. Baby talk at this age can be endearing—for instance, when your child hugs you and says, "I wuv you." It is important, however, that as a parent you serve as a model for correct pronunciation and not imitate the child's speech. However, your child will not be able to immediately say a word correctly just because you do. Correct pronunciation depends both on teaching and developmental capabilities.

There are techniques you can use to develop your child's language abilities. Make a practice of talking to your child in complete sentences. Try to pronounce words as accurately and precisely as possible. If your child uses a short or incomplete sentence, repeat and expand his sentence. Your model provides him with the opportunity to hear longer and more complex sentences. For example, the young child very often says, "Mommy, ice cream." Your response should be something like the following: "Would you like some ice cream?"

As a parent, you have probably noticed how your child gradually learns to pronounce letter sounds correctly. In fact, children are still learning correct pronunciation beyond age eight. In the following chart (which originally appeared in the article "When Are Speech Sounds Learned?" by E.K. Saunders in the *Journal of Speech and Hearing Disorders,* 1972), you'll see the average age estimates and upper age limits in pronouncing letter sounds. The solid line indicates the average age for pronouncing the sound, while the dotted line indicates the age where 90 percent of all children can correctly pronounce it. What is interesting is that some sounds take a longer time to develop in all children than do others.

24

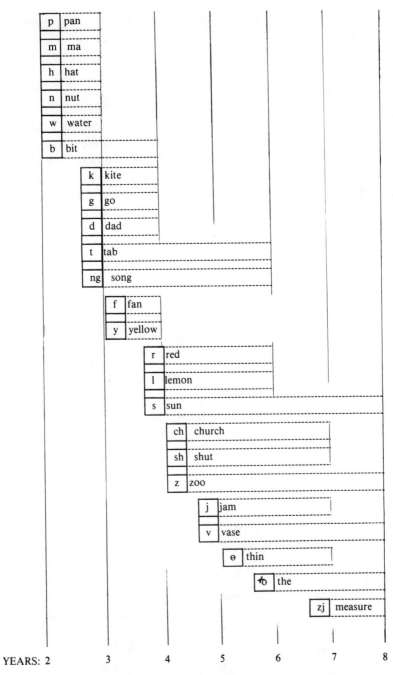

p	pan
m	ma
h	hat
n	nut
w	water
b	bit
k	kite
g	go
d	dad
t	tab
ng	song
f	fan
y	yellow
r	red
l	lemon
s	sun
ch	church
sh	shut
z	zoo
j	jam
v	vase
θ	thin
ƫ	the
zj	measure

YEARS: 2 3 4 5 6 7 8

(From Templin, M., 1957; Wellman, B. et al. 1931)

There are also a number of activities that will expand your child's vocabulary. For example, reading to your child will give him a large number of new words. Spending a day at the zoo and talking about the different animals can increase vocabulary. Discuss how the animals are alike and different, where they live, and what they eat. Baking cookies together can be another excellent activity to increase vocabulary. Naming the different ingredients, cooking utensils, and cooking methods further expands vocabulary. Planting a garden can provide yet another opportunity for adding new words. Talk about the names and parts of plants. Discuss the hows and whys of caring for plants. Everyday experiences can provide many opportunities to encourage your child's growth in language.

Visit your local book store. You'll find some helpful books for increasing your young child's word knowledge. Several publishers have cardboard books containing pictures accompanied by the appropriate word. Enjoy these titles from Price, Stern, and Sloan:

Baby Forest Animals

Baby Pets

Baby Farm Animals

Also, try these cardboard books by Grossett and Dunlap:

Automobiles

A Circus Parade

These books contain stand-up figures but no labels. This gives you and your child an opportunity to give several labels for each stand-up figure.

Another publisher, Tuffy Books, has an interesting way of developing vocabulary. A word or sentence is read, and the child predicts the word being described. In the Tiny Tuffy Book, *Who Am I?*, by T. Tallarico, the sentence clues are, "I put out fires. Who am I?" On the same page a cardboard covering hides the answer. To check his guess, the child pulls open the cardboard cover and finds a fireman. What a good way to get your child actively involved in books! What is especially nice about Tiny Tuffy Books is their size! Any three-year-old can comfortably hold one in his hands.

Can you remember playing "Pat-a-cake, Pat-a-cake" with your baby? As you said the words, you probably helped your child make the movements. Or you may remember doing "Where is Thumbkin?" with your toddler. This and other fingerplay activities set the stage for the development of oral language skills. As your child grows older, you can develop hand and body movements to accompany childhood verses or simple songs. There are a number of fingerplay books that encourage the development of children's speaking skills. Try these books from Price, Stern and Sloan:

> *Wee Sing and Play*
>
> *Wee Sing Around the Campfire*
>
> *Wee Sing Silly Songs*

(These books can be purchased with tapes to help those who don't have musical accompaniment.)

Visual Skills

Another important component of reading readiness is seeing letters and words clearly as well as knowing what they are. (You may hear a teacher refer to this as visual acuity and visual discrimination.)

First, can your child clearly see the letters on the page? This is important! If the letters are fuzzy and run into each other, then your child won't be able to distinguish one word from another or even one letter from another. If your child's vision is normal, then he can learn to discriminate the word "cat" from the word "dog." Seeing likenesses and differences among letters and words is an equally important factor in learning to read. Good clear vision and the ability to tell likenesses and differences in letters and words are necessary for successful reading.

A child usually has normal vision of 20/30 at the age of five. Farsightedness rather than nearsightedness can be a

27

problem for the young child. Therefore, learning to read small print can present difficulties. If your child holds a book too close or rubs his eyes while looking at print, then you may want to consult an eye specialist.

Recognizing differences in letters can be difficult for the young child. Recent studies show that young children, many times, cannot differentiate between letters such as "b" and "d" and words such as "jump" and "clump." At the age of four or five, it is common for a child to write his name, turn the page, and start at the wrong end of the page and write backwards. Lisa, age 5, shows us how easy it is for young children to make this mistake and be totally satisfied with the final product.

When Lisa was asked what was wrong with the writing, she carefully studied it and finally said, "Looks perfect to me," and so it did.

Once the child can see the likenesses and differences among words, he now must learn to commit each word to memory so that each time he sees the word, he can instantly recognize it. It is much easier for young children to learn words that have a unique shape. Most young children will always recognize the word "elephant" in a story, yet have a difficult time remembering words like "when" and "where" or "the" and "then." As you can readily see in the following illustration, the word "elephant" has a unique shape, while the very common words have similar shapes.

Frequently used words are usually very short in length, and the meaning attached to these words tends to be very abstract. Common word shapes, short words, and abstract word meaning make word recognition difficult.

Keeping letters in the correct order within a word is another difficult task for the young child. Has your youngster sometimes read "saw" for "was" or the other way around? Or has he said "on" when the word was "no?" These are normal mistakes for the young reader. For the young child, the sequential order of letters or words tends to be unimportant. As the young child becomes a skilled reader, he will gradually realize that letter and word sequencing is an important aspect of reading. If your child is exhibiting letter or word order confusion beyond age seven or eight, then you should discuss this persistent behavior with his teacher. Until this age, letter and word reversals are quite common and are not considered a serious problem.

To help your child develop good visual skills, talk about likenesses and differences in letters and words. Make his name with cardboard, felt, or magnetic letters and compare it to other family members' names.

Again you should talk about how the names are alike and how they are different. For example, if your child's name is Eddie and other names in your family are Joan, Mark, Carol, and Matt, ask your child if any of the names begin with the same letter. You want your child to begin to differentiate one letter from another. Let him make his own discoveries and rules for seeing likenesses and differences between letters and words.

Matching letters and words is another good exercise to develop visual skills. Your child can make a collage of all the different types of "b's" he can find in magazines and newspapers. Chalk and chalkboard are great for copying letters and words to develop visual skills. Magnetic letters are another means for children to form words. The 3-D letters provide the child with a chance to develop likenesses and differences through touch in addition to sight. Alphabet Teacher by Kiddiecraft is another educational toy to help children recognize likenesses and differences among letters. It can also help your child learn the alphabet. The old stand-by game, Dominoes, is another enjoyable activity to develop your child's visual skills. Out of cardboard, design pieces for the Dominoes game. Divide each piece into two parts. Place one letter or word on each half. Remember to make doubles and triples of letters and words. Play the game the same way you play Dominoes.

Auditory Skills

Another component of reading readiness is your child's ability to hear sounds, identify likenesses and differences between sounds, and to listen and comprehend stories, conversations, et cetera.

Does your child have any loss of hearing? If so, this may cause some difficulties in learning to read. (This is especially true if the primary teacher stresses auditory skills, such as phonics, in teaching reading.) When your child enters school, the school nurse should screen for hearing. If your child has a hearing loss, you will be notified. According to A.J. Harris and E. Sipay in their book, *How to Increase Reading Ability,* here are some possible signals of hearing loss: (1) inflamed or running ears, (2) asking constantly that information be repeated, (3) putting a hand behind the ear to improve hearing, (4) frequently confusing words similar in sound, and (5) unclear speech.

Can your child hear likenesses and differences between words? A child who does not hear the differences between the beginning sound heard in "bad" and that heard in "dad" may exchange one letter for the other. The child would then read the word "bad" as "dad." To become a skilled reader, the young child needs to hear differences and likenesses heard in the beginning (bat, ban), middle (van, rat), and end (red, did) of words.

Listening is another auditory skill important to learning to read. A child must understand a story he hears before he is expected to learn to read. If your child can name the characters, time, place, and explain the story plot, he has a good start for learning to read. From listening, he has learned that books tell something. Something can be learned. Or maybe books cause laughter or tears. But, at any rate, books have messages. For your child to develop good listening ability, he needs to be continually read to. One of the most enjoyable parent-child experiences is the sharing of books, an activity never forgotten and one that can be begun before your child is one year old.

Develop your child's auditory skills by teaching him songs, poems, and rhymes. "Ring Around the Rosy," "Three Blind Mice," and "Humpty Dumpty" are great for young children to hear and learn. Songs, poems, and rhymes help the child hear the rhythm of language and encourage him to be aware of the sounds in language. The wide variety of Mother Goose books and the *Random House Book of Poetry for Children* are favorites of young children. As you read, you and your child can clap out the rhythm to the poem, song, or rhyme.

Develop auditory skills by reading books emphasizing the rhythm of language. The Dr. Seuss books, the Instant Reader Series by Bill Martin (Holt, Rinehart, Winston), and the PSS Surprise Books (Price, Stern, Sloan) are good examples. These types of books can help children develop a keen awareness of English language sounds. Listen to the rhythm in this PSS Surprise Book, *Who's Your Furry Friend?* by Arnold Shapiro.

> Who's your furry friend?
> Is it a moose
> in a bright blue caboose?
> No
> Is it a cow
> who is taking a bow?
> No

Records can also develop auditory skills. There are many enjoyable records for both infants and preschoolers. Both parent and child listen and participate in songs and rhymes. Many of these records include a teaching guide emphasizing finger and body movements. Here are a few interesting records to start you off:

Stewart, G. "Baby Face"
Long Ranch, NJ: Kimbo Education, 1983

Palmer, M. & Palmer, H. "Baby Song"
Freeport, NY: Educational Activities, 1984

Juniak, W. "Put Your Finger in the Air"
Long Ranch, NJ: Kimbo Education, 1982

Smith, Jo "I'm a Delightful Child"
Vida, Oregon: Pacific Cascade, 1977

Pascal, P. & Hearn, J. "Music is Magic"
Highland Park, IL: Sweet Pumpkin, 1982

Games can also help children develop their auditory skills. For example, you can say to your child, "Tell me a word that rhymes with 'cat' and 'bat'." Or, "Do these words have the same beginning sound: 'jet' and 'bed'?" Or, "Tell me a word that begins like the word 'mom'."

When you were a child, can you remember a family member telling you a story? Maybe the story was true or maybe it was pure make-believe. Were you glued to your seat? Did you eagerly listen to each word? Naturally!

Storytelling is an old art that brings smiles and fond memories to all who have experienced it. Storytelling is a wonderful activity for developing listening skills in children, and it's so easy to do. No props or costumes are needed. All you need is a good story that you know by heart. Begin by telling stories that have happened to family members. Then try your hand at telling familiar tales like "Goldilocks and the Three Bears" or "The Gingerbread Boy." These all-time favorites help develop your child's sense of story. As he learns to read, he'll look for certain familiar story elements like setting, characters, and plot. Consequently, he will have a head start in comprehending stories.

Directional Skills

When a book is open, does your child know where to begin? Does he know to begin with the left page rather than the right? Do his eyes focus on the top left of the page? Do his eyes move from left to right as you read across the print? The young child needs to learn these skills if he is to become a skilled reader. Your child does not need to know the labels—left, right, top and bottom. But he needs to know the concept. How do you know that he has developed this concept? Just observe him while you read aloud. Watch his eye movements. Do his eyes follow your voice as you read from left to right? While listening to his favorite books, does your child follow the print with his finger? Directionality is not an automatic skill. It needs to be taught.

You can help your child develop directional skills by pointing to the top of the page when you begin reading. As you read, slide your finger beneath the print. When you finish reading the line of print, lift your finger off the page. Move your finger again, left to right, on the next line. Do not let your finger make a return sweep by going right to left along the page. This may confuse the child. You want your child to understand that one reads from top to bottom and left to right. Do not worry about encouraging finger pointing while reading. The young child needs to use his finger to keep his place and develop his sense of direction. As the child develops into a skilled reader, he will stop using his finger.

Experiential Background

Experiences are one of the most important steps for learning to read. To understand a story, the young child has to have many varied experiences. Both direct and indirect experiences help the child learn more from books. If your child has never been to a city and has never traveled on a bus or train, how can he easily understand the characters' feelings and daily events within the story? Reading to your child and showing pictures are good examples of indirect experiences that children need for better comprehension. Planting seeds and observing growth, building structures out of clay, sand, etc., tasting different kinds of food are good instances of direct experience that will lay the foundation for developing understanding from books.

Every day you and your child share many wonderful enjoyable experiences. Try to make each new experience better than the last one. Instead of merely picking a bouquet of flowers, point out the names of the flowers or the names of fish caught for dinner. While taking a walk, talk about some of the things you see. While sharing a book, point out new objects in the pictures. As your child dresses, identify the different colors in his clothing. As he plays with his trucks and cars, point out the different parts like the wheel, axle, tail pipes, et cetera. Making the effort and taking the time to share experiences will benefit learning and help develop a closer bond between you and your child.

Interest

The last item of reading readiness — and a very important one — is the child's interest in learning to read. Is your child interested in books? Does he pick them up and look at the pictures? Does he make up a story to go with the pictures in the book? Does he like you to read to him? Does he want to know what words "say?" Does he like to read with you? If you can answer yes to some of these questions, your child is interested in print and probably is looking forward to learning to read. Interest in learning is the key, and you, as a parent, should keep encouraging his interest in books.

Reading to your child as well as reading for your own enjoyment can increase your child's interest in reading. Going to the grocery market and pointing out to your child what the different labels "say" can further encourage awareness of print. Reading the signs on the road while you drive is a natural way to develop the young child's interest. You will see a big smile the first time he recognizes a sign that points to a nearby McDonald's.

The world is full of print. Make your child aware of it and compliment him on the ability to recognize words in his environment. Even if they may not always be the exact words, he is developing a notion of what reading is all about. The young child learns to read by understanding first what should be on the sign, label, or page, and then progresses to identifying the precise words in print. Your praise for each attempt at reading will make him more interested in learning how to read. The next time your youngster says "Hamburgers!" when he sees the McDonald's arches, smile and let him know you are happy with his attempt at reading.

Is my child ready to read?

Does a young child have to master each of these readiness skills before he can learn to read? No. What children do need is to be exposed daily to each of these skills. Children develop language by talking every day with adults and other children. They learn to identify letters and words by seeing and talking about the print found in our world. Sounds are learned by listening and playing with the rhythm of our language. Directional skills are developed through daily discussions and simple games. Visiting a variety of places and talking about new objects help the young child with reading. And, most important, reading yourself and reading to your child will create a growing interest in learning to read.

The mystery of reading readiness has led educators into conflict for the last 20 years. All of these skills are necessary for learning to read. Yet teaching the subparts to children does not guarantee that a child will become a successful, much less an early, reader. How then does a child learn to read? One of the ways researchers examine this process is by studying children who have taught themselves to read before they began kindergarten or first grade.

Early Readers

Let's look at the child who begins to read prior to school without any formal training. This child has progressed beyond the reading readiness stage and has taught himself how to read. Early readers have fascinated parents and educators for years. The early reader breaks the written code on his own by periodically posing questions such as "What does this word say?" and "How do you spell my name?" Curiosity, motivation, and knowledge of concepts are some of the elements that bring about early reading.

The early reader learns to read similar to the way he has learned to talk. When a child learns to talk, he is exposed to a great number of words, varied pronunciations, and numerous sentence structures. Think about the many different words a child hears in everyday conversation. The young child hears various pronunciations of the same word due to the numerous accents found in our mobile society. By listening to a radio or television program, the child hears a variety of dialects. Sentence structure does not greatly limit the young child. In fact, research has shown that when most children enter school, they are able to produce most of the sentence structures found in their native language. However, they are still developing and increasing their ability to produce more complex language. The young child is faced with a vast amount of language information — sounds, grammar, and vocabulary. He is able to sort through this large amount of information and produce grammatically correct and intelligible sentences.

Let's look at the similarities between learning to talk and learning to read. The early reader uses his skills of oral language to help him learn to read. Just as the young child learns to speak, so does the early reader learn to read by immersing himself in language. But, in this case, it is written language. In her research on early readers, Delores Durkin found that early readers were intrigued with print. They copied, wrote, and asked questions about words. Generally, Durkin has found that early readers were curious, encouraged by parents to continue their investigation of print, and read to regularly. The parents took the time to answer their children's questions about print. Usually there were older brothers and sisters willing and able to help the younger sister or brother with reading.

You may think these children came from affluent families and had high IQs. Not so! Children of all economic classes were early readers. Durkin identified 14 percent as upper-middle, 31 percent as lower-middle, 53 percent as upper-lower, and 2 percent as lower-lower. Nor were early readers necessarily children with superior IQs. A broad range of intelligence levels were found. Neither boys nor girls were more likely to be early readers. Other characteristics of early readers were the child's persistence, conscientiousness, and self-reliance.

In another report, Eunice Price reports that parents found their children "obsessed" by the written word. The child would ask what words said, would look for recognizable words, and would read all day long. Some parents said this obsession drove them to distraction, but other families of these early readers had a high regard for reading and were patient while answering their children's questions about reading.

The early reader understands the relationships among oral language, print, and meaning. They know a message is hidden in print that needs to be unlocked. Faced with vast amounts of printed information, the early reader makes sense of the print via his own daily activities and his ability to question. The explosion of new information is no different for learning to read than it was for learning to talk. In both cases, the child is able to put ideas together to make sense of language.

What Should Parents Do?

Delores Durkin, in her study of early readers, commented that parents often apologized for their children's achievement. They were concerned that their first-grade children might be bored and confused in school. Parents even second-guessed themselves by posing questions like the following: "Should I have ignored my child's questions about words?" (Parental concern was understandable after ideas were voiced in the late 50s that warned them not to teach their preschoolers to read.)

Educational beliefs changed with the times. Research in the 70s not only substantiated the learning abilities of young children, but encouraged parental involvement as an important factor. In the 80s, parents are being asked to take an active role in their child's learning. Schools are beginning to recognize the importance of developing a strong parent-teacher partnership in children's learning.

Preparing You as a Partner

Your first questions may be *when* and *how* should I teach my child to read?

When?

Awareness of *when* your child is ready to read is most important. You can determine this by answering the following questions. Do not skip to numbers eight and nine if the answers to numbers one through seven are no.

1. Does your child have an interest in learning new things? Do you expose your child to a variety of learning experiences in order to motivate him?

2. Does your child enjoy books? Does he enjoy sitting and listening to a story read to him?

3. Is your child aware of the print in his environment? Does he ask you questions like "What does that word 'say'?" Does your child "read" symbols such as stop signs, McDonald's arches, pictures, et cetera?

4. Does your child usually speak in complete sentences? Does your child have an average-size vocabulary for his age? (An average three-year-old knows approximately 1,000 words.)

5. Does your child see similarities and differences in objects? A child cannot see differences in letters or words if he cannot see differences in objects.

6. Does your child play games with language either with or without your help? Can he supply the final words in nursery rhymes, identify opposites, rhyme words, et cetera?

7. Does your child feel good about himself? Research has shown that a child's self-confidence and self-esteem are connected to his reading achievement. This has to do with the fact that when a child does not learn to read, he feels bad about himself and his ability to succeed.

8. Does your child recognize the letters of the alphabet? Are they in sequence? Flash cards are not needed for this analysis. Walk down a street and find an "M" on a sign, read a book and find a "d" on a page.

9. Does your child know that letters have sounds associated with them? Again, flash cards are not needed. Play sound and word games. ("Look around the room and tell me all the words that have the beginning sound heard in these words: 'bat,' 'band,' 'book'.")

If your child is able to do six of these nine points, he should be ready and successful at learning to read. Now the second question: *How* can you help your child learn to read?

How?

First, provide your child with an environment that encourages reading. Your home should contain a wide variety of reading materials, such as fiction and nonfiction books, magazines, and newspapers. Your child should see you reading daily and discussing what you have read with other members of the family. One of the characteristics of the home environments of early readers is that family members read, and at least one parent is an avid reader. The parent is an important role model to the preschool child. It is during this stage of development that the young child wants to learn how to do adult tasks. Often you'll see your child "copying" or wanting to do your daily chores. Can you remember buying your child a toy lawn mower? As you mowed the lawn, he'd follow with his toy mower. The same thing will happen if you read regularly. Your child will sit down and read, even if it means he is only looking at pictures. What a wonderful beginning to reading!

Your child is "ready" — now what?

Step 1: Motivation

To further whet your child's reading appetite, read daily to him. There are many good picture books your child will enjoy hearing. You will find a list of books for children of preschool age through junior high on page 241. This list is meant only to get you started and is by no means a complete listing of the many wonderful children's books.

There are also source books to help you select additional books for your child. Nancy Larrick's *A Parent's Guide to Children's Reading* (5th Ed.) is an invaluable source for parents. She reviews many children's books and provides parents with helpful hints about reading to children. Other good source books are NCTE's publication, *Adventuring With Books;* Zena Sutherland's book, *The Best in Children's Books;* and *Reading Ladders for Human Relations,* published by the American Council on Education.

These books can help you make better critical choices when selecting books for your child. Source books for children's literature serve only as guides for book selection — your best guide for selecting books is your own child. Even your youngest can find books in your local library that he would love to hear read aloud. You and your child can have a wonderful experience exploring new books at the public library. While selecting books together, describe the different stories in each book. Your child will be excited that you know about different book characters. He enjoys knowing that you have read these books and want to share them. You will find selecting and sharing books to be a rewarding parental experience.

After selecting some good books, how can you effectively read these books aloud to your child? Here are some helpful ideas. For the first few books you read aloud to your child, let your child hold the book with you while you read it aloud. Holding the book will get him involved in the reading act. It also allows the child to see the illustrations and print found in books. This can be the beginning of helping your child to form a concept about books and reading. The child will begin to understand that print "says" something, and reading is another way to communicate. You are now starting to lay the groundwork for getting your child to read.

Step 2: Knowing More about Books

As your child becomes more interested in books, you can point to the words as you read. Make sure your child sees you start reading on the left-hand page, at the top of the page, and at the left side of the page. Use your finger to show him directionality while reading. By using this procedure, you help your child develop appropriate directional movement for reading. Do not insist that your child pay such close attention to your finger movement along the page that he loses his desire to listen to stories. You are then defeating your purpose. If you continually read with your child using the appropriate directional movement, he will learn the left-to-right direction needed for reading.

As you read aloud to your child, you want to be sure he is comprehending the story. To check your child's understanding, informally ask questions before, during, and after you have read the book aloud. Questions asked prior to the reading help your child develop a purpose for listening. Pre-reading questions should help the child focus on the main idea of the story. For example, in *The Tale of Peter Rabbit,* a main idea question might focus on what happened to Peter Rabbit when he did not follow his mother's rules.

Questions during the reading can focus on predicting what may happen next in the story. Eric Carle's book *The Very Hungry Caterpillar* is a good story in which young children can predict what will happen as the story progresses. Carle's story about a caterpillar that transforms into a butterfly provides the child with many opportunities to predict what the caterpillar will do. For this story, a good question for prediction is, "What do you think the caterpillar is going to eat next?" Questions that ask children to predict motivate children to listen to the rest of the story.

You will also want to ask questions after reading the story. Some of your questions should focus on your child's feelings toward the story and characters. Dare Wright's book *The Lonely Doll* spurs children to talk about Mr. Bear's kindness towards the homeless Edith. Young children can easily answer questions like: "How do you feel about Mr. Bear's promise to Edith?" "What do you think about Edith?" "Do you think Edith and Little Bear deserved a spanking?"

Other questions should center on your child's basic understanding of the story. Questions asking *who, what, where, when, why,* and *how* are good for developing your child's understanding of the story. Be careful that you do not ask too many questions and squelch his interest in books. The beginning stages of teaching reading should be relaxed and enjoyable.

All types of picture books should be read to your youngster. As mentioned earlier, Mother Goose is an old favorite and provides children with the opportunity to learn the natural rhythm of language. Rhymes are also easily memorized, and you and your child can "read" the poem together as you point to the words.

ABC books can help your child learn the alphabet and the familiar objects that begin with a specific letter. Key words usually accompany each letter of the alphabet which will help the child memorize and recall these words in other printed materials. Alphabet books usually contain both the upper and lower case letters which help children realize that both black marks "B" and "b" stand for the letter "b." These are only a few interesting ABC books:

> Alexander, A. *ABC of Cars and Trucks*
> Fife, D. *Adam's ABC*
> Garten, J. *The Alphabet Tale*
> Johnson, C. *Harold's ABC*

Concept books introduce abstract relationships to children that can facilitate reading comprehension. Topics such as time, size, distance, prepositions (for example, "over," "under"), emotions, etc. are covered. Learning abstract relationships can further develop language skills and is an important skill for reading comprehension. In one concept book, *Over, Under and Through* by Tana Hoban, children learn through detailed illustrations the meaning of these three words: "over," "under," and "through."

Cardboard, plastic, and cloth books are very good for the infant and very young child. These books usually can withstand much abuse. Water, dirt, food, etc. can be easily washed off. For the baby, plastic "bathtub" books are popular. Few words or sentences are found in these books. The main purpose is to familiarize the youngest with books so they become a natural part of his life.

Another favorite for babies is cloth books. These books are soft and contain pictures with little or no print. Cloth books allow the infant to cuddle up and enjoy the feeling and touching of books.

Toddlers will enjoy cardboard books. Nice colorful pictures abound with a limited number of words and sentences. Some cardboard books ask for the child's participation. Pop-up books fall into this category. As you read the story aloud, your child is asked to pull or push a tab to see something new in a picture. Preschoolers enjoy the pop-up activity, and it keeps their attention. Some good informative pop-up books are published by

Franklin Watts. *Animal Families* includes information about specific animals, such as koala bears and tree squirrels. *Wonders of Nature* contains information on day and night, seasons, et cetera.

Two other interesting cardboard books, Little Brown's *Mystery Picture Book* series and Dial *Playbooks,* also encourage preschoolers to be active while listening or reading. The *Mystery Picture Book* series require the child to pick out objects in pictures after reading each page. Books in this series are:

> *Where's My Hat?*
> *Search for Sam*
> *Find the Canary*

Dial *Playbooks* have cards and a gameboard to go along with the story. Each page asks the child to match a game card with a picture from the story. Books in this series are:

> *Alligator's Garden*
> *The House That Bear Built*
> *Monkey's Marching Band*

Cardboard books will create hours of enjoyment for you and your child.

Select books that have repetitive verses such as Verna Aardema's *Who's in Rabbit's House?* ©1977, published by E.P. Dutton (Dial). Throughout the book, the rabbit and other animals try to find out who has taken over the rabbit's home. The different animals always ask this question: "Who's in rabbit's house?" The repeated reply from the intruding animal is, "I am the long one. I eat trees and trample on elephants. Go away or I'll trample on you." Young children can easily learn the words to this verse and are able to "read" it when it appears in print. By reading, I mean memorization, but this is an important first step in learning how to read.

With all books, children will want to hear their favorites over and over again, a good sign of awakened interest, and parents should be willing to reread these books. From each rereading, the child learns more about the story and develops greater familiarity with the words in the book. Have you ever read a book to your child for the tenth time and substituted or added a word? What does your child say? In most cases, your child stops you and tells you the correct word. Not only are listening skills being developed, but the child is learning that a book always contains the same words even after ten readings. From rereading, your child will identify words he sees on signs, labels, et cetera. He will even begin to recognize these words in other stories.

Step 3: The Writing and Reading of Stories

The child learns to read easiest by reading stories about his own experiences. A child can remember words as well as be motivated to read when he is reading about something that happened to him. The vocabulary and sentence structures are the child's and therefore easier to read. This is called the Language Experience Approach or LEA. The child tells or dictates a story to an adult or older child who writes it onto paper. Gradually, the child learns to read the story back to the adult.

In order for your child to dictate a story, he has to have something to talk about. A good starter for dictation is asking the child to write a letter to grandmother and grandfather telling about playing at the park. Here's a typical dictation from a child about playing at the park.

> Dear Grandmother and Grandfather,
> We walked to the park.
> Mama and I went on the swings.
> I went on the slide and the monkey bars.
> Love, Matthew

Usually your child's first dictations will be short. Write down the exact words he says. The words should be printed in upper and lower case on "primary" paper. This type of paper can usually be found in all local drug stores or stationery stores. Primary paper has larger spaces so a child can read and write easily (see next page). It contains three lines to use as a guide for printing words.

The purpose of exact dictation is to help your child read the printed material with the greatest amount of ease. When you change his words or sentence structures, you have removed the cues your child needs when reading his dictated story. By changing his language, you are subtly saying to your child, "I have a better way of saying it than you do." This non-acceptance of your child's language patterns may affect his self-esteem and his desire to dictate future stories.

Your child may enjoy dictating stories about books you have read together. Read a picture book to your child and discuss the story with him. When you feel he has sufficiently talked about the book, invite him to dictate something about the story. The dictation may take many forms. It may be a recap of the story, a new adventure for one of the characters, or your child's feelings about the story. Whatever your child dictates, accept it and make him feel good about his work. After he has finished his dictation, read it back to him, making these two comments: "Give me a name for your story and tell me if you want anything changed." These two comments are quite important to reading and writing. You are teaching your child about the main idea and about editing. After he has given a title and approved his work, then you and he should read the dictation together—perhaps several times. Now he is prepared to read the story with some assistance. As your child reads his dictation, underline the words he knows. Those words he cannot identify should be immediately supplied. This will help him develop meaning and eliminate frustration. Encourage your child to draw a picture to accompany his story. Hang the story and picture in a prominent place so others can see his masterpiece. Your child will then realize that you take pride in his work, and this helps to promote motivation and self-esteem.

The next day ask your child to read his dictation. Again, underline those words he recognizes and immediately supply those words he does not know. Use a colored pencil to differentiate words known now from those recognized yesterday. The words he remembers a day later should go into a "word bank," a container of known words. Use any household container for your child's word bank. Write each word your child recognizes a day later on a 3" x 5" index card. Place these word cards in the container or word bank. Each time your child dictates a story and rereads it at least a day later, there will be words he recognizes, and these known words are also to be added to his word bank. Add any other words he can readily read, such as his name, other family members' names, et cetera. Words placed in a word bank must be easily recognized by your child. If they are not, your child will become frustrated when you do reading activities with the word bank.

Keep a folder for your child's dictated stories. Each new story should be dated and placed in his folder. By keeping all dictation, you can provide many opportunities for reading practice. You will find that your child will enjoy rereading his stories over and over and will increase the number of words he can read on his own.

Step 4: Developing a Reading Vocabulary

Once your child has approximately 200 words in his word bank, you are ready to try some reading activities. Here is a list of word bank activities you and your child can do together.

1. Make sentences with the word cards.

2. Alphabetize words into envelopes marked with a single alphabet letter (for example, "a").

3. Find all the words that have the same beginning sound.

4. Choose word bank cards that have common spelling patterns in our English language, such

as "sat," "met," "sit," "hot," and "take," "ride," "bike," "kite." Use the word bank card as the key word for developing rhyming words that have the same spelling pattern. Write down on a piece of paper the rhyming words your child tells you. He'll begin to see common spelling patterns found in the English language.

5. Build word concepts (for example, opposites: big-small; pretty-ugly, tall-short). Select a word from the word bank and ask your child to tell you a word that means the opposite. Write the word down so your child can see it in print.

6. Select a word bank card and have your child draw a picture describing its meaning. Or select a word bank card and ask your child to dictate a sentence explaining the meaning of the word.

7. Match word bank cards with words found in the child's dictated stories or in magazines.

8. Use word bank cards to write a new story.

9. Select a word bank card that describes a person, animal, or a feeling.

10. Select some words from the word bank and copy them on paper or use letters to form the words.

These are only some of the many activities you and your child can do with the word bank. Go ahead and create some new activities and vary some of the suggested activities.

Vocabulary can be learned by using dictated materials. Ask the child to point out words he knows from his dictated story. This question usually brings instant success. The parent can eventually make the task more difficult. For example, have the child find a word when given the definition. "What words in your story begin with the sound heard at the beginning of these words: 'fan,' 'fat,' and 'fit'?" A more difficult task would have the child find the words with the same beginning, middle, or ending sound as heard in "mat." If a task is too difficult, return to an easier one. The development of vocabulary is achieved through meaningful experiences and from the child's own language. Whenever you or your child are reading his dictated stories, use your finger to point out each word as well as the left to right direction of print. While your child is trying to read his own dictated story, he will need your assistance to identify the words. Always be encouraging and supply the unknown words or say, "Here is the unknown word. This sentence tells us what else was in the garden. Can you read it now?" A personal experience can bring meaning to the written word and help in recognizing it.

Another helpful strategy for identifying unknown words is to read to the end of the sentence and then make an attempt at identifying the unknown word. The context of the sentence can provide additional clues for word identification. The example below indicates how this strategy works. The unknown word is underlined. The dotted line underneath the sentence indicates that your child should read to the end of the sentence and say "blank" for the unknown word. He can return to the beginning of the sentence and attempt to identify the unknown word and continue reading.

Edith promised not to be bad.
\------------------------------------->

This procedure helps the child concentrate on reading for meaning.

You may also find that your child forgets words that have been placed in his word bank. Do not become distressed and feel that he is failing. In learning, the child does not continually progress nor learn at the same pace. At the beginning of learning to read, your child learns words quite quickly; then after awhile it seems he has not learned any new words for a long period of time and may even have forgotten some words previously learned. This is normal and should be expected. Then, suddenly, he may increase his word knowledge by leaps and bounds, only again to reach a plateau. However, this is quite normal. It is important that you do not push your child so reading becomes unpleasant. Many children do not like endless activities centered on a few words. Adjust your reading activities to fit the needs of your child. Some children only enjoy dictating stories, which is also beneficial to reading development. Others enjoy rereading their dictations.

Good ideas for dictation focus on your child's personal experiences (for example, things I love best, things that scare me, a favorite TV show, places we visited, et cetera). Make sure you discuss the experience prior to any dictation, for this is the key to good LEA stories.

Step 5: Progressing to Independent Writing

At some point your child will be able to move from dictation to writing his own stories. Once your child feels comfortable with dictation, he should be encouraged, but not forced, to write his own stories. When are children able to write on their own? If your child knows how to write his alphabet, can relate sounds to letters, and shows an interest in writing, then he is ready to begin writing. Once your child writes, encourage him to use invented spellings—that is, to spell the word the way it sounds. You may find that your child is anxious about spelling a word correctly. It is best to tell him to spell a "word" the way it "sounds." At this stage, the purpose of writing is to communicate ideas, not spell perfectly. Spelling correction comes later. Don't worry that your child won't learn to spell words correctly. Research has indicated that as children grow older, their invented spellings change to correctly spelled words.

After your child writes a story, ask him to read it to you. Praise him for his good work. At a later time, you may rewrite his story using standard spellings. Then have him reread his story, checking to see if he can read the standard spellings. You may have to help him read certain words. Don't be alarmed! He is just learning. Keep his writing in his folder so he can keep rereading it.

Suggestions for Parents

1. Introduce your child to books in which the author discusses your child's hobby, interests, or new experiences. Factual books can develop a whole new world for your child. New horizons can be opened or further expanded. After your child reads a book about his hobby, interest, or new experience, a discussion can take place. Emphasize what your child already knew about the topic and what new, same, or conflicting information was developed by the author. These discussions should help your child connect his knowledge with that of the author's, and comprehension should be improved.

2. Make puppets together and have your child dictate a script for a puppet play. Then perform the play for the entire family and your child's friends.

3. Here are some additional topics for LEA:
   - Use family photographs to stimulate dictation or writing.
   - Use the series "Write Your Own Story" (Dover Juvenile Books), a coloring book to encourage dictation or writing.
   - Use sequenced cardboard picture books entitled *Jasmine and the Cat* and *Jasmine's Bedtime* published by Child's Play. The sequenced events will help your child dictate or write a story.

4. Caption books can be another stimulating reading activity. Choose magazine pictures based on one topic, such as animals. Paste one animal picture on a piece of colored paper. Staple pictures together to make a book. Talk about each picture so your child has some information about the animal. Ask your child to provide one or more sentences about the picture. Print his sentence(s) on paper. Repeat these

steps until the book is finished. Reread each page at regular intervals.

5. Making books from your child's dictated stories can be an enjoyable activity and adds permanency to your child's work. It allows for many rereadings without tearing or damaging. Children also enjoy seeing their stories made into books. They feel like real authors.

   Making books can be simple or elaborate. Harvey Weiss's *How to Make Your Own Book* provides a variety of ways for making children's books. Or try this simple bookmaking project:

   Step 1: Cut two pieces of cardboard larger than the pages of your child's dictation.

   Step 2: Cut one large piece of contact paper so a one-inch border surrounds all four sides. This will serve as the book's cover.

   Step 3: Staple together the pages of your child's story. Use a large number of staples so the pages are firmly held together.

   Step 4: Cut contact paper at each corner so it can neatly fit around the cardboard cover.

   Step 5: Lift plastic sheet off contact paper so adhesive shows.

   Step 6: Place cardboard covers on contact paper leaving one-inch borders around all four sides.

   Step 7: Fold the cut corners and sides around cardboard so all edges are covered.

   Step 8: Place stapled story between the two covers. Make sure one inch of adhesive is firmly pressed to the front page and one inch of adhesive is pressed to the back page. This allows for a stronger binding. Your child now has his very own book.

6. Go to the library and select the *I Can Read Books* published by Harper Row. These books are meant for children from ages 4-8 and enable the child to learn to read a story with ease.

7. Check out library records with the books' dialogue. These recordings are made with famous professional voices, and your child should enjoy them.

8. Use a pizza board and cut out two rectangular areas. Place a verb in the middle of the board. Using a brad, attach a slightly larger circular piece of paper with nouns to the back of the pizza board. Your child can turn the bigger circle and practice reading each new sentence. A model is provided below.

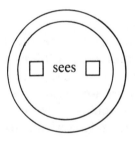

9. Make repetitive books. Use your child's name, a verb, and a fill-in space for each book page. Let your child dictate a word for each fill-in and draw a picture to correspond with the sentence meaning.

10. Label objects in your child's room or in your home. Your child can learn to associate the word with the object.

Chapter 3

STARTING SCHOOL—
A POSITIVE APPROACH

In a popular children's book entitled *Rufus M,* author Eleanor Estes creates a delightful character, Rufus, who is about to enter first grade. It is a summer day and Rufus' older brother and sister are busily involved in reading and do not want to be bothered. Rufus' mother is busy in the kitchen, leaving no one to play with him. He asks his sister and brother to go to the library with him, but they have just come back from the library and aren't interested.

Rufus decides to take his scooter and go to the library to check out his own book. On the way to the library, he resolves to check out a "Brownie" book just like the ones his sister and brother are reading. As he enters the library, the librarian frowns at him—his hands are dirty! Before Rufus can advance one more step, the librarian marches him off to wash his hands. With hands as clean as a whistle, Rufus can finally search the shelves for the precious "Brownie" books. His eyes quickly spot the Brownie figure on the book's spine. Ah, at last, he can now read the same books his brother and sister enjoy. However, Rufus does not have a library card, and, to make matters even worse, he cannot write his own name to get one. In fact, Rufus can't even read.

This begins Rufus' adventure to obtain a library card so he can "read" books like his sister and brother. In this episode of *Rufus M,* Estes captures young children's need and desire to learn and accomplish the tasks older youngsters and parents can do.

During the ages of 6-11, children are especially interested in learning to do things like adults. This is the stage of development when children want to learn "how to work," and are still willing participants in tasks such as mowing the lawn, washing the dishes, planting gardens, working on cars, and learning to read—especially if an adult will work alongside of them. Erik Erikson, a developmental psychologist, describes this stage of development as a time when children deal with the conflict of industry versus inferiority. Erikson summarizes this stage in five words, "I am what I learn."

The child's conflict is in learning to be successful without an over-abundance of failure experiences that can lead to withdrawal and giving up. Too much discouragement with new tasks, such as learning to read, can cause children to feel inferior and result in hostility or nonparticipation. It is this stage of development in which children need to be challenged, but only to the point where they do not lose their self-confidence.

These are the years during which children want to learn how to do things and to figure out how things work. Remember the day you returned from grocery shopping, and your youngsters decided they were going to be helpful and bake a cake or fix your lawn mower? But, instead, what a mess! Children see the world of work as an enjoyable investigation. As they learn new things, they compare their projects or learnings to other children their age, in this way evaluating themselves through self-comparison. They also measure their accomplishments through their friend's approval. But, at this age, approval from parents and other adults is of the greatest importance. Throughout this stage, Erikson suggests to parents that they recognize and applaud children's accomplishments in order that their children can achieve a positive solution to the conflict of industry versus inferiority.

Parent feedback is one form of approval and recognition that enhances learning. Feedback need not only be in the form of praise. Children need both positive and corrective feedback to learn. The important thing to remember is that children's accomplishments need to be acknowledged and discussed rather than to be labeled "good or bad" because of successes or failures.

The child who makes his dad a letter holder should not only be praised for his effort, but should be asked how he did it. The child who reads a book should be praised for reading another book. However, it's the added parent interest in what the child learned from the book that may encourage him to continue reading. As the child discusses the book, you may find him confused about something he read. This is the time to provide assistance and corrective feedback.

Corrective feedback is appropriate and can promote learning if harsh criticism and "put-downs" are avoided. Comments like "You mean you have not learned that at your age?" or "Don't you understand that by now?" should be avoided. It's easy to make these remarks, but they can be harmful to your child's ego. You can best help your child learn by showing interest, enthusiasm, support, and recognition as he attempts new tasks. Praise him for his best efforts! The old adage "Nothing succeeds like success" is practical and true. As a parent, you can provide this feeling of success through your time, genuine interest, and continual efforts.

The Relationship of Learning and Development

What is a beginning reader between the ages of five and seven capable of learning? The most suitable approach for a young child's thinking is through the Language Experience Approach (LEA), the dictation and reading of his own stories. Unfortunately, many popular magazines, newspapers, and parent books say that beginning reading instruction should start with the teaching of phonics. Phonics is an important part of reading, but it should not be the first kind of instruction young people receive. First of all, children who begin sounding out words do not understand that the major goal of reading is to understand. Also, sounding out words tends to take the joy out of reading. In a phonics approach, children are not focusing on the delightful characters or story line. Young children will grow tired of instruction lacking in meaningful and enjoyable experiences, and there is still another problem with the initial teaching of phonics that goes beyond meaning and enjoyment. This is the child's inability to think in complex, abstract terms required in learning many phonic principles.

Young Children's Thinking Abilities

Children's thinking is affected by their personal experiences or environment and their stage of development loosely defined by the child's chronological age. The child's stage of development and personal experiences set the limits of learning during beginning reading instruction. Learning can be speeded up to an extent but there are limits to what a child can do and learn. His capabilities are limited by his stage of thinking development.

Jean Piaget is a recognized authority in children's thinking. According to Piaget, most children entering kindergarten and first grade are in the pre-operational stage of thinking which begins at approximately age two and continues to approximately age seven. Piaget explains that the pre-operational child does not see the world in the same way adults do, and his reasoning abilities are quite different from that of an adult. For example, a six-year-old can't solve the following problem: Two rows of chips are placed in front of the child. Both rows have the same number of chips. In each row, the chips are placed in direct horizontal and vertical relationship to each other as shown in the following illustration.

0   0   0   0   0   0
0   0   0   0   0   0

If asked, the child agrees that the number of chips in the first row is the same number as in the second row. In the following illustration, the *number* of chips in each row are not changed, but only moved so that there is no direct horizontal and vertical relationship.

0   0   0   0   0   0
  0 0 0 0 0 0

The child now says there are more chips in the first row than the second because he focuses on length to determine which row has the greater number of chips. At this age, the young child is unable to focus on both length and number. Therefore, he doesn't realize his error.

The child from age five to seven has difficulty focusing on two things at once to determine an answer. As a result, his thinking seems illogical to adults. But, in fact, the child's thinking is logical. He just can't put all the information together to develop the correct answer. If your child is seven or younger, try the chips experiment. At age seven, you may find that the child is able to look at both number and length to determine the correct answer because he is learning how to use more than one piece of information to come up with a correct answer.

Your next question may be the following: "Can you train a child to see the world in a logical adult manner?" Learning can be accelerated up to a point. But it is still bound by the sequential stages of development that all children must systematically pass through. To a degree, the parent or teacher can stimulate and speed up concept development, but there are limitations to the amount of acceleration that can be achieved. Researchers have tried to teach children perceptual concepts, like the chips experiment, that go beyond their stage of development. In most cases, the researcher has been successful at teaching the correct answer to a single experimental task, but the child's ability to make this transfer to other tasks has been a failure.

If children do not perceive the world in the same way as adults, how does this affect reading instruction? Let us look at phonics instruction, which is often one of the first approaches to beginning reading. In phonics, children have to understand relationships between the letters and sounds of the English language. One of the goals of phonics instruction is for the child to correctly associate the sound with the letter. If our language had only one sound associated with each letter, young children would probably have less difficulty learning phonics. Their thinking abilities would allow them to focus on one bit of information to develop a correct answer. However, the English language often has more than one sound associated with a letter. Let us look at the words below that appear frequently in beginning readers.

two, too, to, blue, flew, you, shoe, fruit

The "u" sound in the words "too," "to," "blue," and "flew" have different letters associated with the same sound. In fact, there are eight different letters or letter combinations associated with this one sound. Do you think the young beginning reader can easily understand this concept? In my opinion, the young child would not and may become so confused that he ends up guessing, being wrong, and becoming frustrated—not a good feeling for the beginning reader!

You may think the "u" sound is not that common. Let's look at the letter "a" and see the number of sounds that can be associated with it. Consider these words:

have, father, a, head, laugh, play, fat

These are very common words in a beginning reader's vocabulary. If these words are taught by phonics, the young reader of 5-7 would again be totally confused by the number of different sounds associated with one alphabet letter. Which sound does one choose? Does this mean that the young reader shouldn't be taught phonics? No, it means the young child ought to be taught those parts of phonics that have only one sound associated with a letter. Most of the consonant sounds are associated with only one alphabet letter. For example, "b" as in "bed," "d" as in "dad," and "f" as in "feather." There are letter combinations that also have a single sound association. The consonant clusters like "ch" in "children," "sh" in "shelf," "str" in "street," "spl" in "splash," etc. all fall in this category. Any of these phonic clusters with a consistent one-to-one sound and letter correspondence are easier for young children to understand and learn.

The vowel sounds associated with the letters a, e, i, o, u, and other vowel combinations have multiple sound associations that are difficult for young children to understand and learn. It is usually not until the latter part of age seven or older that children can begin to understand multiple sound associations—for example, the letter "a" can have the sound of long "a" as in "cane" or short "a" as in "cat." When children can readily understand multiple sound associations, then it is fine to teach this area of phonics.

To teach your youngster some phonics, follow the activities presented on pages 70 and 71 and teach only those letters that have a single sound association. It is always good to remember that phonics is an essential part of learning to read, but only one small part. Never let your child lose sight of the fact that reading is for understanding and enjoyment.

Around ages seven or eight, youngsters enter what has been called the concrete operational stage of development. This stage of thinking continues to develop until age eleven or twelve, and, again, this age range is only approximate. The child now begins to think more like an adult although his logical thinking is limited by his own observations. The child can make logical decisions when he can play with objects and see what is happening to the objects. Learning by seeing and doing facilitates understanding. For example, reading becomes a concrete learning experience when the child fingerpaints, dictates a story about painting, and then learns to read his own story.

During the concrete operational stage of development, the child can classify and relate ideas and concepts to objects and activities. The concrete operational child is now able to understand that one object can be classified under two or more areas, but his thinking is still limited to direct observation. Discussing classification of objects without seeing or doing it can still be difficult for the child of seven through twelve. This aged youngster needs to do or see what is being classified. Discussion is not a concrete experience, and a child's understanding and learning can be hindered.

Let's consider how reading instruction can be made concrete. Make word cards for common household objects. Tape the cards to the objects. You or your child can demonstrate and discuss the use(s) of each object. After several objects have been introduced, remove the labels and mix them up. Let your child choose a label and match it with the appropriate object. Ask your child to demonstrate how the object works. Encourage him to provide a sentence or two so you can write it down. Ask him to read those sentences at a later date. This activity promotes active learning. The child is learning to read the names of objects he can see, feel, and manipulate.

The Brain's Role in Learning

The brain is not passive, but active. It selects, interprets, organizes, and remembers information from the environment. The brain interprets, for example, what the eye sees. Thus, when a child reads, it is not the eye that selects the next word to be read and understood—it is the brain that makes such selections and interpretations, selections and interpretations that are either accepted, rejected, or modified due to previous learning. Once information is taken in, it is placed into a previously organized system. Therefore, it is important that, as a parent, you relate new information to your child's old, familiar learnings. Otherwise, the new information is not likely to be remembered.

Let's apply this concept to reading. Your child is reading a story in which people barter for goods and services, but he has no experience or knowledge about bartering and so will most likely experience difficulty in comprehending this story. To provide him with information, you need to relate a familiar experience similar to the idea of bartering. What child has not traded one of his toys for a friend's toy! Discussing this experience will help your child relate the familiar with the unfamiliar. Now as your child reads, he will develop a better understanding of the events in the story.

The brain not only takes in and organizes information, it also has the ability to remember and recall information. The brain's ability to remember and recall can be compared to a computer. The right word, phrase, or thought helps the child recall earlier learnings just as the right command prompts the computer to call up information. But children are not computers, and many times previously learned information is not easily recalled. Unless earlier learning is recalled, a child's learning potential is lessened. However, instruction can play an important role in aiding recall and enhancing learning.

Let's refer to the story about bartering. To help your child understand bartering, you discussed previous personal experiences about bartering. This helped your child relate familiar information to the new information presented in the story. To help your child remember and recall the concept of bartering, provide additional experiences related to previous instruction. For example, play a game with the whole family. Each family member has a service or product another person needs. If there is no money, how can each person acquire the services and products he needs? Of course, by bartering! Use a real life situation. Your child wants to go to the baseball game, but he has no way of getting there. You need your car washed. How can both of you achieve your goal? Set up other situations so your child develops the concept of bartering in a concrete fashion.

Instructional activities can trigger previously learned information and make the child conscious of what he knows. It also provides additional exposures to the same concept. As we all know, repetition increases the understanding and learning of a new concept. The end result will be your child's increased ability to remember and recall information easily.

Putting Your Knowledge into Practice

Let's review some of the important aspects for teaching a six- to eight-year-old child to read.

- Activities should make the child an active participant in developing reading skills. Remember, the child of this age learns best by using concrete objects and personal experiences.

- New information should be related to something the child already knows well.

- Many and varied experiences are needed to help children remember and recall new information.

- A variety of activities illustrating the same concept will firmly establish this concept in the child's mind.

- As you teach your child to read, make sure he is successful and is enjoying himself. When he shows signs of frustration and repeatedly fails an activity, stop and do something else. Continued failure and frustration can be counterproductive to learning.

Now let's look at some specific reading activities for the six- to eight-year-old. Start with activities one, two, and three if your youngster is not yet reading. Activity one is for all children whether they are reading or not. Don't forget—the reading activities suggested in the previous chapter can also be used with this older child.

1. Read to your child every day. It is best if your child selects the books you are to read aloud. But add some of your own selections and include all types of literature, such as folk tales, poetry and biographies.

2. Select some simple books, such as John Burningham's books: *The Baby, The Rabbit, The Friend, The School, The Snow, The Dog, The Blanket,* and *The Cupboard.* Then, use poster board to make an oversized book containing the same number of pages as the original. On each piece of poster board print only the words that appear on one page so the "big book" looks exactly like the smaller version. Do not draw the illustrations. Let the child do this. After completing construction of the "big book," you and your child can share the enjoyment of learning to read it. First, read it aloud to him and point to each word as you read it. Make sure you are not reading it in a slow word-by-word fashion, but in a natural conversational pace. After you have read it a few times to your child, ask him to read it along with you as you point to each word. Once your child has some confidence with the "big book," let him read and point to each word by himself. You may need to provide some of the words for him but remember he is only a beginner. Discuss each page so your child can later draw a picture to go along with it that will express the meaning of the page. Drawing pictures shows your child the importance of reading for meaning. When the "big books" are reread, the pictures can help him identify words.

After your child has success with the "big book," let him read it whenever he chooses and encourage him to point as he reads to ensure that he is correctly associating the read word with the printed word.

Select simple predictable books to make "big books." Predictable books have very few words per page, words and phrases are repeated frequently, and the story is easily anticipated. In a predictable book, the child can easily guess what will happen because a logical sequence of events is presented. The predictable story sequence then helps the child identify the words on the page. Let's look at an example of what predictable books can be like.

The Circus

Our family went to the circus.
We saw tigers.
We saw elephants.
We saw zebras.
We saw lions.
We laughed at the clowns.
We ate popcorn and candy.
We had a wonderful day at the circus.
Our family will go to the circus again.

Notice that the story is very short. There is only one sentence per page, each sentence has few words, and the content is very predictable. This story relates to most young children's experiences and makes prediction easy and success high.

Other predictable books are Jane Belk Moncure's *What Does Word Bird See?* and *Word Bird's Hats.* In each of these books, sentences are repeated within the story. This makes it easier for the child to predict the words in the text.

Predictable books may also emphasize the rhythm of the language. *Ten Apples on Top* and others by Dr. Seuss capitalize on the rhythm of language. Here are a few excerpts from *Ten Apples on Top* by T. Le Seig (Random House, 1961). Listen to the rhythm as you read.

"Look! See now.
I can hop
with four apples
up on top."

"And I can hop
up on a tree
with four apples
up on me."

"Look here you two
See here, you two
I can get five
on top.
Can you?"

As your child progresses, you will want to select more difficult predictable books with more words and sentences per page and more pages per book.

3. In one sitting, read four to six predictable books to your child. As you read, point to each word and encourage your child to join you in reading. Each day reread the same books and add another predictable book to your reading time. Repeated reading of the same books helps your child become familiar with the story and words, and he will easily be able to read along with you once he has heard the story several times. By reading a variety of books and by introducing a new book at each session, you can combat boredom, both the child's and yours. Once your child can read and point to words on a page, you can remove this book from your reading time and add a new one. Now let your child read the known books to you and the rest of the family. Performance time is necessary for motivation, self-confidence, and continual development.

4. Learning the verses to songs and singing them is an enjoyable learning experience for you and your child. Songs develop the natural rhythm of language so necessary for beginning reading. There are many good children's song books in your local library. You may find the following list helpful.

Children's Song Books

Jim Along, Josie: A Collection of Folk Songs and Singing Games for Young Children. Compiled by Nancy and John Langstaff. New York: Harcourt Brace Jovanovich, 1970.

The Fireside Book of Fun & Game Songs. Collected and edited by Marie Winn. New York: Simon and Schuster, 1974.

Eye Winker Tom Tinker Chin Chopper: Fifty Musical Fingerplays. By Tom Glazer. New York: Doubleday, 1973.

5. Wordless picture books are a good means to encourage children to talk and create their own stories. You may want to start this activity by telling your child that the book has no words, but still tells a story. Tell your child to create a story by looking at the first picture and continuing to the end of the book. After your child has looked at the entire book, let him talk about the story, write his version on paper and use it for reading material. The following wordless picture books may help you begin this activity:

Alexander, Martha. *Out! Out! Out!* New York: Dial Press, 1968.

Goodall, John S. *Paddy's New Hat.* New York: Atheneum, Margaret K. McElderry Book, 1980.

Mayer, Mercer. *Frog, Where Are You?* New York: Dial Press, 1969.

Turkle, Burton. *Deep in the Forest.* New York: E.P. Dutton, 1976.

6. Puppetry is a good way to teach children to read. First, select some easy short plays from children's magazines or library sources. Read the play to your child and together make puppets for the different characters. Puppets can be easily made from socks, ice cream sticks, paper bags, et cetera. Scenery or an elaborate puppet stage is not necessary. Your child will enjoy reading and acting out the characters in the play.

7. Using pictures and objects can help increase your child's listening, speaking, and reading vocabulary. Cut out pictures from magazines and write the word that identifies them below each picture. The pictures and words can be placed in a loose-leaf notebook that will serve as a homemade dictionary. Your child can glue in words and corresponding pictures and place them in alphabetical order. Writing or dictating a sentence about the meaning of the word will further increase word meaning. Pages can be easily added to a loose-leaf notebook so

the dictionary can be continually expanded. You may want to use a published dictionary as a model to familiarize your child with this valuable learning tool.

8. After your child has read a book, have him draw a picture of his favorite event in the story. Ask him to explain it, and later pose some quesions to develop his thinking skills. To start the discussion, try this question: "Why was this your favorite part of the story?"

9. Choose some books that tell how to make something or how to perform a task. *Betty Crocker's Cook Book for Children* is an excellent book to get children actively involved in reading. Start with a simple recipe that requires no cooking. First demonstrate to your child how to read and follow the recipe directions to make a specific dish. Then encourage your child to help you with another simple recipe. Eventually, let your child try an easy recipe on his own, but under your supervision. Your child will have a sense of satisfaction when he can produce something as a result of his reading. Other books that involve making and doing projects are:

Gibbons, Gail. *Things to Make and Do for Your Birthday.* New York: Franklin Watts, 1978.

Weiss, Ellen. *Things to Make and Do for Christmas.* New York: Franklin Watts, 1980.

Supranger, Robyn. *Merry Christmas! Things to Make and Do.* Mahwah, N.J.: Troll Associates, 1981.

Stein, Sara Bonnett. *The Kid's Kitchen Takeover.* New York: Workman Publishing Co., 1975.

Fiarotta, Phyllis. *Snips & Snails & Walnut Whales: Nature Crafts for Children.* New York: Workman Publishing Co., 1975.

Rockwell, Harlow. *I Did It.* New York: Macmillan, 1974.

10. Help your child select some easy library books or magazine stories. Set a purpose for each story or book your child reads, such as "What do you think the story is going to be about?" A purpose-setting question provides

a focus for understanding the story and helps to improve your child's reading. After your child has finished reading the selected story, ask him to answer the purpose-setting question. Pose some additional questions about important facts of the story. Also, include questions requiring your child to make inferences and develop critical thinking.

Inferential questions require your child to interpret what the author says. For example, in the story *The Three Little Pigs,* a typical inferential question would be the following: Was the one little pig's straw house very strong and sturdy? The author doesn't explicitly tell us the answer to the question but he provides many clues to an acceptable answer. Thus, the reader has to interpret the author's ideas.

A critical thinking question requires your child to make a judgment and support it with facts and logic. A question from *The Three Little Pigs* that requires critical thinking is: In which house would you want to live? Why?

If your child has difficulties answering any of your questions, provide some additional clues. Refer him to the page or pages on which the question is answered. If this doesn't help, show him where the information is found. See if he can then explain the answer. If not, explain how this part of the story answers the question. By explaining how you found the answer, you will help your child with future questions.

11. You can begin to teach children at ages seven or eight about vowels (a, e, i, o and u). Children at this age are now apt to understand that a letter can have more than one sound associated with it. But before you begin teaching the vowels, check to see if your child knows the consonant sounds at the beginning and the end of words. Here is a list of the consonants: b, c, d, f, g, h, j, k, l, m, n, p, q, r, s, t, v, w, x, y, and z. You can easily check your child's knowledge of consonants by using the following method: "Tell me another word that has the same beginning sound as these words: 'box,' 'boat,' 'bath,' 'bike.' "

Your child should respond with one or two words with the same beginning sound. Continue this method with the other consonants. Then repeat the procedure with the consonant sounds at the end of words. If your child has difficulty with this, try some of the following activities.

   a.   For a racetrack game, construct an oval track like the one in the illustration. Establish a starting and an end point for play. Make cards to fit each marked space along the track.

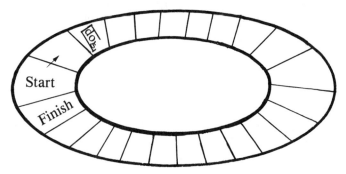

On each card, print a one-syllable word beginning with a consonant sound, such as "dog." Each card should be a word your child knows. Place one card on each space of the game board. Make another set of cards with different one-syllable words beginning with a consonant sound. Place the second set of cards face down in the center of the board. To begin play, each player takes seven cards from the center and places the cards face up. Use a single die to move players around the racetrack. When a player lands on a space, he discards one or more word cards that have the same beginning sound as the one on the space on the game board. As he discards, he says the two words to show they have the same beginning sounds. If the player does not have at least one match, then he must draw a card from the center pile. Play continues until the first player arrives at the finish line, or one player runs out of playing cards. Each player counts up the number of cards left in his possession. The player with the fewest cards wins the game. You will be able to think up variations of this game.

b. A picture collage can be made for each of the consonant sounds in which your child is having difficulty. Use magazines and newspapers for the collage.

    c. A variation of the popular Bingo game can help your child learn consonant sounds. Make several cards like the one illustrated below.

P	H	O	N	I	C	S
man	red	hut	gas	tip	fed	bat
pin	fat	sit	kit	cut	jam	rot
cub	tip	ran	let	get	pot	dig
pet	dog	bed	not	hat	tin	win

Place a single syllable word on each space. Make small cards with a single syllable word on each card. Turn the cards over. Select a word card and say the word. Each player covers a word having the same beginning (or ending) as the called word. Play continues until one person has covered one line of words going across or down on the game card.

After your child knows the consonant sounds, you may want to try the above activities with consonant clusters. A cluster can be two or more letters whose individual sounds are combined into a blended sound, such as in the words "splash" (spl), "street" (str), "tree" (tr). A list of some of the common consonant clusters is: bl, cl, gl, sl, cr, dr, fr, pr, tr, gr, tw, sc, sm, sw, scr, spr, spl, str, pl. Another type of cluster is one sound associated with two letters, as in these words: "thin" (th), "child" (ch), "shut" (sh). Here is a list of this type of cluster: ch, sh, th, ng, ph, wh.

Try this additional activity with consonant clusters. Make two cubes out of heavy paper as illustrated below. Fold and tape at the edges. Place a single consonant cluster on each face of one cube. On the other cube, place on each face the final letters of a one-syllable word with a blank preceeding it (for example, __an, __un, __ue, __op). Roll both cubes and say the word by blending the cluster with the final letters of the one-syllable word.

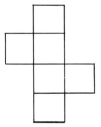

After your child has had success with consonant sounds and clusters, you may begin to familiarize him with short vowel sounds. Use words with high frequency spelling patterns such as "cat," "bed," "tin," "hot" and "tub." This spelling pattern is known as consonant-short vowel-consonant (cvc), and it has consistent pronunciation. For teaching vowel sounds, try Word Sort developed by D. Morris. For this activity, make one-by-two inch cards and write a single cvc word on each card, such as "mat." For the first few times of playing Word Sort, choose only two vowels to classify, such as "ran" and "set." To begin Word Sort, place one cvc word, such as the word "set," into a column. Place a different cvc patterned word, such as "ran," into a second column. (See illustration below.) Pronounce and point to each word.

Select a word card, then pronounce and point to the words in both columns. Look at the selected word card, pronounce it, and place it in the appropriate column. An example is provided below.

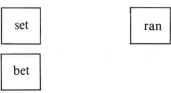

72

Repeat this process one more time. Now let your child choose a word card and follow the same steps.

Classify these two patterned words a few times until your child is classifying the words fairly quickly. Now add a new column using the short "o" pattern as in "hot." Once your child becomes proficient with a three-patterned sort, you can add a fourth pattern. Keep adding columns, until you have covered all the vowel sounds (a, e, i, o, u). Word Sort provides the young child with an opportunity to be actively involved with concrete objects which is so necessary for learning.

There are other vowel patterns that can help children to read. The long vowel pattern (consonant, long vowel, consonant, silent "e") (cv̄c¢) is also very consistent. What do you notice about long vowels in this spelling pattern: "lake, "bike," "bone," and "cute?" The long vowel sounds "like" the alphabet letter.

Use Word Sort to contrast the long pattern (cv̄c¢) with the short pattern (cv̆c). Begin by using one cv̆c pattern and one cv̄c¢ pattern as shown below.

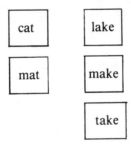

cat	lake
mat	make
	take

After your child can readily understand the difference between these two "a" patterned words, then add other vowels. Keep playing Word Sort until your child automatically classifies words into their appropriate categories.

Another vowel pattern that can be helpful for your child is the r-controlled vowels, as in the words "fur," "bird," and "arm." In r-controlled vowels, the "r" sound affects the sound of the vowel. To teach the r-controlled pattern, use Word Sort and introduce this pattern as you did the other vowel patterns.

Remember, in order for phonics to be an effective skill, children have to apply it. When your child comes to an unknown word in a story, give him time to apply his phonics skills. To help him do this, keep your Word Sort cards handy while your child reads a story. When he comes to a vowel patterned word he can't pronounce, place the appropriate Word Sort card above the unknown word. Ask your child to pronounce the Word Sort card, and then attempt the unknown word. If he still can't recognize the unknown word, show him how the two words are alike. Next pronounce the word on the card and apply it to the unknown word. Your encouragement and help in applying what he has learned can help your child become a skilled reader.

These final activities are for children who are well beyond the beginning stages of reading.

12. Cut apart comic strips and have him sequence them.

13. Ask your child to read a short story from children's magazines and identify the most important point the author wanted the reader to learn.

Should Kindergartners Be Taught to Read?

Should reading be taught in kindergarten? Or is kindergarten the place and time for developing socialization skills? These two questions are always posed in opposition of each other as if only one choice can be made. Developing the young child's socialization and reading skills can both be accomplished. The most important question in learning to read in kindergarten is being ignored. Can the child learn to read with success?

If your kindergartner has had no exposure to reading, then review the nine points in the section entitled "When?" in Chapter Two. If you can answer yes to question one as well as six of the nine questions, your child can begin learning to read. Begin instruction by following steps one through five in Chapter Two. If your kindergartner is reading or is about to read, then encourage him to continue. Use the activities suggested in this chapter as well as those in Chapter Two.

Kindergarten Reading Program

The teacher should informally identify three groups of students — those who can read, those who have familiarity with reading, and those who have little or no experiences with reading. With this knowledge, the teacher can plan appropriate learning experiences. The child who is reading needs continual exposure to a wide variety of books. Both the classroom and the school library should offer a large selection of books to your child, and the kindergarten teacher should encourage your child to select and read books on his own so he can continue to develop his reading skills. For both the child who is already reading and the one about to read, there is a need to develop their own reading materials based on personal experiences. Just as you and your child developed reading materials from his oral dictation or writing, the teacher should also use this approach in her classroom. The Language Experience Approach (LEA) discussed in Chapter Two has been a part of kindergarten programs since the 1800s.

In the kindergarten classroom, LEA may be group dictation rather than individual dictation due to the large number of children and the small amount of instructional time. In group dictation, each child may contribute only one sentence to the story rather than dictating the entire story, but all of the children will use the group dictation for reading material. As a parent, you may find your child unable to read the group story as readily as his own dictation. This is understandable since not every word has been dictated by him. Mastering reading from group experience stories may take longer.

Besides oral dictation in LEA, your child's instructional time should be spent on composing and writing his own stories. The teacher may retype the stories, correc-

75

ting the spelling when necessary, and may use them as another source of reading materials. Or the teacher may display the child's original work, recognizing that children are unable to spell accurately at this age. Oral language activities should be integrated with reading. Kindergartners can share the stories they have read with others. They can describe the parts they liked the best or the least.

Puppetry can be an important part of the kindergarten reading program. Children can make and use puppets to present a story they have read. Role playing and other drama activities should be used. This gives children an opportunity to talk and think about stories. It also gives them a chance to explain what they have learned from reading.

Every kindergarten reading program should include some time for listening to the teacher read aloud. A variety of literature should be read to these youngsters, such as fantasy, folk tales, poetry, realistic fiction, et cetera.

One caution: Many commercial kindergarten reading programs emphasize phonics in teaching reading. In fact, the major or only component to the program is learning letters, sounds, and words. Little or no attention is paid to reading for meaning. As discussed earlier, learning phonics tends to be a very abstract skill for young children. Phonics should never be the major focus of a kindergarten reading program. These youngsters need to understand that reading is a meaningful activity like talking. Focusing on sounding out words or learning each sound of each letter without reading or listening to good literature is boring and confusing for young children. Generally, phonics should play a minor role in the total kindergarten reading program. As the child becomes a reader, he can begin to see the importance of identifying unknown words through sounding out words. But phonics is better understood and better developed in first and second grade. As a parent, you need to know what is being taught in your child's classroom. Ask the teacher to explain the kindergarten reading program.

A Kindergarten Program for Non-Readers

The kindergartner who is not reading should be exposed to oral language activities, such as show and tell, puppetry, role playing, et cetera. These youngsters need to be read to. They need to hear and see print. They need to be exposed to many different kinds of literature: fantasy, folk tales, poetry, realistic fiction. These children need to hear the rhythm of language, the predictability within a story. They need many opportunities to talk about stories. Following oral directions, retelling a story, and answering questions about a story are necessary for successful beginning reading. They should be playing games with rhyming words, listening and repeating sentences, as in the game "Telephone." Pre-readers need to listen and memorize rhymes and poems. Activities like labeling classroom objects and seeing and learning words for the days of the week and the months of the year prepare a child for reading. Another good activity for pre-readers is dictating a phrase or sentence to go along with a picture. These kinds of listening and speaking activities will better prepare the kindergartner for formal reading instruction.

No Single Method for Learning to Read

Over the years different methods have been identified as the one and only successful method for teaching children to read. Even today there are those who still claim that a single method can teach all children to read. From research, we know there is *no one method* that is successful with all children. In 1963 a government-funded project was undertaken to identify the best approach for teaching children to read. The various types of reading methods were pitted against each other. The results were that no one method was found to be superior to another. In the final analysis, it was the teacher who made the difference in the child's learning to read.

What are the major reading methods used in schools today? We're going to look at the three main types:

language experience, basal readers, and phonics and will discuss the advantages and disadvantages of each.

Language Experience Approach (LEA)

Language experience has been fully described in Chapter Two. This method is based on teaching children to read by using the child's own oral language and personal experiences. The child knows his story because he dictated it. Supposedly, this makes reading an easier task. The child's reading vocabulary and story content is limited only by his oral vocabulary and experiences. During the primary years, children's oral vocabulary is much larger than their reading vocabulary, and the Language Experience Approach doesn't limit the number of words children can learn.

Word bank activities that accompany LEA are more easily accomplished by a parent and child than in a classroom situation because it is one-to-one instruction. In classroom group dictation, each child must cope with a new and different set of words. Consequently, different activities for each child may need to be planned. Dictation can also be a time-consuming activity, and teachers see children for only a limited time. Thus, LEA is demanding and sometimes looked upon as a luxury rather than a necessity.

Basal Readers

Basal readers are widely used in the United States. In fact, almost 90 percent of our schools use them. Basal readers are commercially published programs for children in kindergarten through the eighth grade which usually consist of a student reader, workbook, worksheets, and teacher's manual for each grade. Most basals try to teach word identification skills, such as phonics, as well as comprehension and study skills. The readers contain fiction and nonfiction stories to be read by the students. The teacher primarily uses workbooks and worksheets to teach specific reading skills, such as phonics, factual comprehension, et cetera. The major thrust of basal readers is to teach reading skills, thus supposedly creating competent readers.

In beginning reading books, there is a limited number of words or what educators call a "controlled vocabulary." The disadvantage of controlled vocabulary is that each child is limited to the number of new words he can learn. The number of words may be too small for some children and too large and frustrating for others. As a parent, you may have already experienced another disadvantage—your bright second-grader is reading book J, and your third-grader, who has reading difficulties, is reading from the same book. The self-concept of your third-grader is deflated, and his motivation probably negatively affected. The basal reader doesn't appropriately address the individual needs of children who are either poor or high-achieving readers. If your child reads on grade level, then the basal tends to be more satisfactory. The major advantage to a basal reading program is its systematic method of teaching children to read from kindergarten through eighth grade. Its overall system for introducing and practicing the program's reading skills is well organized. In a basal program, children are taught many reading skills but may, in fact, be taught many more than what is necessary for competence.

Phonics

Some commercial programs emphasize phonics as the main avenue for learning. The program may look like a basal reader since children have readers, workbooks, and worksheets, but the main emphasis is on phonics. The philosophy of the program is: If children can "break the code," they can read. According to this program, to "break the code" or say the words, the non-reader has to learn phonics. In some of these phonic-oriented programs, children are taught nonsense words. The goal is to be able to associate the correct sound to the letter or spelling pattern of the English language. For example, the following words or non-words may appear in a list for children to pronounce: "bat," "cat," "dat," "gat," "hat." Children learn to read stories that make little or no sense. Rhyming and pronouncing regular patterns of words is the main goal. A typical example of a beginning reader follows below:

> Jan ran.
> Jan ran to man.
> Man ran to Jan.
> Jan fans the man.
> The man fans Jan.
> Can Jan fan the man?

At the beginning stages of reading, young children are not asked to understand what they read. It is assumed that the main problem in learning to read is figuring out the written language code. Supporters of a phonics-only approach maintain that children who understand oral conversation can read and understand written language and that the problem the beginning reader has to overcome is saying the words. However, we all probably know of children — and maybe adults — who can say the words on the page, but who do not understand the message behind the words. This is also true for beginning readers. If young children are not taught from the beginning that reading has to make sense, then children learn to attend only to pronunciation. They won't understand the purpose for learning to read. Mastering phonics is only one of many skills. Thus, the main disadvantage of these phonic programs is their heavy emphasis on teaching one skill and their lack of attention in developing comprehension.

Other commercial phonic programs are supplementary and usually appear in a workbook, worksheet, or a kit format (tapes, manipulative objects, et cetera). These programs are meant to give children additional opportunities to learn phonics. Their main disadvantage is that many of these programs are not coordinated with the systematic instruction provided by the classroom teacher.

New labels are given to old concepts previously developed in the classroom. For example, the teacher calls the vowel sound in "cat" a short "a" while the supplementary program calls this an "unglided" sound. Confusion develops and children stop using phonics. Supplementary phonics programs can be good, but teachers must make sure the concepts and vocabulary are used in the same manner as they are taught in the main reading program.

A Diverse Approach to Reading

Since there is no *one* best approach to teaching children to read, experienced teachers currently use the best from each of several approaches. As a result, the teacher now has to be knowledgeable about a variety of reading approaches and materials. In a varied reading program, no single approach is used. LEA, basal, and phonics are all taught. One approach may be emphasized over another due to an individual child's strengths and weaknesses. Hopefully, your child's school draws on all of the various techniques to teach reading.

Establishing a Parent-Teacher Partnership

The first contact with your child's teacher, in many ways, is the most important. This is the time you are building rapport and developing a relationship of trust. Therefore, an appropriate time and setting is important for the first brief encounter. A phone call, a note, or, best of all, an initial face-to-face meeting is best. A good time to contact your child's teacher is during the first week of school. This gives you an opportunity to meet one another when neither has any complaints. Otherwise, the first teacher contact can be unpleasant. The teacher is usually calling to describe some unacceptable behavior or report a child's lack of progress and her concern that a learning problem may exist. This kind of contact usually puts a parent on the defensive, and communication can be hampered. Neither party wins, and the biggest loser is your child.

However, during the first week of school, the teacher probably knows very little about your child. Thus, you are in a position to provide some helpful information. This is the time to mention that your child either can or cannot read. If your child can read, describe some of the books he has read. If your child lacks certain skills, then identify these. And, last but not least, assure the teacher that she has your full support and cooperation. Provide the teacher with your phone number and tell her to feel free to call when help is needed from home. Let the teacher know from the start that you want to work with her, not against her, so your child will learn. Do not feel you are intruding or asking for special treatment. You are simply indicating that you are truly concerned that your child receives a good education.

After your child has spent six weeks in school, again call or drop a note to check on your child's progress. If a conference needs to be set up, do it immediately. Even if your child is doing well, you may still want a conference. If your child is in kindergarten or first-grade, the following questions may be the most appropriate:

1. Is my child able to get along with others?
2. Can my child participate well in group activities?
3. What can I do to encourage or help my child learn to read?
4. Can you describe my child's reading program?

In second and third grade you may want to ask these additional questions:

5. Is my child experiencing difficulty with any specific skills? If so, what are they? How can we help him with these skills?
6. Is my child experiencing any difficulty that may hinder learning in the future?

If your child is experiencing difficulty in school, make

sure you do not become defensive. Try not to allow your own ego to be affected when your child is not doing well in school. Even though it is hard as a parent to be objective, it is important that you and your child's teacher work together in a cooperative, not a competitive, manner. You must have faith that the teacher is doing a good job teaching your child. Parents and teachers need to be teammates if difficulties are to be effectively overcome. Find out immediately how you can help your child. Ask the teacher to make specific suggestions, such as reading activities, tutoring, testing, et cetera. Always keep abreast of what is happening in school. It is important to your child's future.

Parent-Teacher Organizations

Every school has an organization for parents and teachers. Some are nationally affiliated and some are not. But in either case, it is an excellent way to understand how the school works. It also provides a good opportunity to know your child's teacher better. Parent-teacher organizations can be a means for change and continued school improvement. Within the organization, there are committees on which parents can voluntarily serve classroom teachers, librarians, or learning center directors. As a volunteer, you can receive a better understanding of your child's school program because you will be a part of that program. This is a good way to build a relationship of trust between you and your child's teacher. Now the two of you are working together.

Not all parents are able to volunteer during school hours. However, there are other opportunities to become involved in a child's schooling. Music programs, science fairs, plays, etc. are great activities for parent involvement. Such activities are beneficial to your child's learning and can develop a good working relationship with your child's teacher. Try to get involved with your child's school and parent-teacher organization. It can be another way to help your child in school.

Suggestions for Parents

1. After your child reads a book, suggest he make a book jacket depicting a major story event or an overview. Your child may enjoy experimenting with the art medium used by the book's illustrator. If the illustrator uses collage, let your child choose an event from the story and interpret the event by using collage.

2. When your child enters school, he should have his very own library card. Go to the library together to apply for one.

3. Keep reading to your child even if your child is reading by himself. You are a good "model" for fluent reading and your child still needs to hear good oral reading. Reading aloud also provides an opportunity to develop listening skills and positively affects his reading development.

4. Order children's magazines for your child's reading pleasure. Together decide which magazines are of interest to him.

"One thing in your favor—with these grades,
you couldn't possibly be cheating."

Chapter 4

BUILDING READING POWER

By the time your child has reached fourth grade, he has probably learned how to read and has developed some proficiency with a number of reading skills. Most likely he can automatically recognize many printed words. He has the ability to sound out unknown words, use the context to identify new words, and understand the author's ideas. Your child is well on his way to becoming a skilled reader. His job during the middle grades (4-8) is to continue on this same road of learning. He'll be sharpening his reading skills and learning how to gather information from books, magazines, and newspapers. This period of a child's schooling is aptly classified as "reading to learn" rather than "learning to read." Your child's goal is to become skilled at learning from printed materials.

The Growth in Children's Thinking

Some time around the end of elementary school (grades 6-8) children's thinking skills advance. The adolescent is beginning to learn to think abstractly. He may be able to reach conclusions without actually trying out or performing his ideas.

Since thinking and reasoning without doing is still a difficult task for many adolescents, instruction should still include time for adolescents to learn by "doing." Imagining and discussing new ideas and concepts without "doing" may hinder learning and cause frustration.

Consider your child's thinking abilities in each subject area: science, social studies, mathematics, and literature. Does your child think abstractly in some areas like mathematics yet is unable to use this kind of thinking in science? Why does this occur? Many times your child has acquired many math-related experiences and lots of mathematical knowledge that give him the extra ability in mathematics to think in the abstract, but in science, he may have little knowledge and few experiences, thus hindering abstract reasoning. What can you, as a parent, do to advance your child's thinking? You can provide a variety of experiences and opportunities to acquire knowledge in many subject areas! For example, develop abstract thinking by making simple electrical circuits and talking about the logical steps and theory of electricity. Eventually, he'll develop concepts through imagining and discussing rather than by making projects and doing experiments.

Broadening of Reading Skills

Comprehension

Once children can say the words on the page, are they automatically comprehending? Many children may understand the basic ideas of the passage, but miss the author's intricate relationships. Comprehension is a complex process involving four major factors: thinking, experiential knowledge, reading skills, and attention.

To comprehend, the reader is required to think and reason while reading. A good reader develops a meaningful picture while reading text. At the same time, he is combining his personal experiences with the author's ideas. To comprehend, the reader is also applying his reading skills, such as oral language skills, vocabulary knowledge, phonics, directionality, et cetera. Comprehension also requires the reader's attention while reading. The good reader gives his complete attention to reading and doesn't think about other things. Your child's goal is to develop proficiency in all four of these areas: thinking, experiential knowledge, reading skills, and attention. Comprehension can be nurtured by both teachers and parents. Discussing books they have read can stimulate children's thinking and reasoning. Parents can sharpen children's thinking by comparing and contrasting the facts and ideas from TV and radio news reports, magazines, and newspapers. Family discussions centering around current events can be an interesting and ongoing project. This activity not only develops thinking skills, but brings the family together to discuss relevant events and today's world problems. Include all family members in the discussion no matter what their level of understanding may be. Encourage your children to ask questions so they develop knowledge, understanding, and comprehension of the event. Factual questions are important, but so are questions requiring children to make inferences, judgments, and applications. Factual questions usually are the who, what, where, when, and why type. Inferential questions ask the reader to focus on what the author seems to say. Applied and judgment type of questions require the reader to go beyond the author's ideas to evaluate some of the concepts learned while reading. Parents can use the number and quality of questions asked to gauge their children's knowledge and involvement in a discussion. The more questions they ask, the greater their understanding of the subject. As you may have experienced yourself, the more you know, the more you ask.

To help your child with question asking, model factual, interpretive, and applied levels of questions. Reading activities such as Radio Reading and Request (described in *Reading Strategies and Practices* by R. Tierney, J.

87

Readence, and E. Dishner. Allyn and Bacon, 1980) use modeling as a way of teaching questioning. These activities can help your child sharpen his question-asking skills as well as his comprehension. Radio Reading is easy and fun to do with your child. It is based on the analogy of a radio announcer and an audience in which the reader reads a short selection while the audience listens. After the reading is completed, the reader asks questions about the selection. Both parent and child take turns reading aloud and asking questions. The parent's role is to model good question-asking skills. Different levels of questions should be posed so the child has the opportunity to develop various levels of thinking. From this activity, the child learns to ask and answer questions and improves his oral-reading skills. Selections from local newspapers and children's magazines are perfect for this activity. They are short and contain interesting and relevant articles for children.

The Request activity also develops your child's ability to ask questions. Select an interesting short story or book to share with your child. Both of you will read the first sentence. Then tell your child to ask any questions he wishes about the first sentence. Your role is to answer the questions in a straightforward manner. For this activity, don't tell your child to look up a word in the dictionary or to "sound out" an unknown word. After your child has asked all his questions, you take a turn at question-asking. Your questions should develop more complex thinking and understanding. Try to use inferential, judgment, and application questions. When you complete your questions, you both will read the second sentence. Again, take turns asking each other questions. The questions can include all the previously read material. This questioning pattern repeats until you feel your child has enough understanding of the reading selection to continue on his own. For variation, you can read a paragraph rather than a sentence before asking each other questions. The purpose of this activity is to develop good question-asking skills as well as provide background knowledge for better comprehension.

You'll find that not all of the questions can be answered from reading the selection. You and your child may need to look up answers in additional sources. Look things up together so your child learns how to find answers in other places. If you insist that your child look up answers on his own, the Request activity will probably lose its appeal. Some of the questions may have no answers. This is not uncommon, and children need to realize that not all questions can be answered.

There are many other comprehension activities you and your child can do together. Remember not to force your child into any of these activities. Reading experiences should be enjoyable, not intolerable or frustrating. The goal is not only to help your child become a better reader, but to encourage reading so he will become a lifelong reader.

Here are a few more comprehension activities:

1. Choose a recipe from a cookbook and try creating the masterpiece together. Discuss the importance of following directions exactly. Explain the abbreviations used in the recipe. Discuss the recipe's vocabulary by showing the objects or by illustrating the cooking technique.

2. Encourage your child to select a variety of reading materials, such as magazines and newspapers. Encourage him to read different types of literature, such as science fiction, nonfiction, mysteries, poetry, et cetera. Reading aloud various forms of writing may be a good way to awaken your child's interest in a new subject. It can also provide background knowledge for better comprehension in the future.

3. Building model airplanes, birdfeeders, letter holders, etc. promotes comprehension. Children need to read and follow the directions closely so the end result is successful. You and your child can begin the project together to help him get started. Once he is able, let him read the directions and do the project himself.

4. An enjoyable comprehension activity is the Directed Reading-Thinking Activity (DRTA) (described in *The Language-Experience Approach to the Teaching of Reading* by R.G. Stauffer. Harper & Row, 1970). The DRTA challenges children's thinking by requiring children to predict what is going to happen in the text. For example, tell your child to read only the title of a story and predict what the story is going to be about. After he makes a prediction, tell him to read to a certain page to find out if his prediction is correct. When he finishes reading the assigned section, ask him if his prediction is accurate or inaccurate. He should then read or tell the part that supports his prediction. Now ask him to predict what the next part of the selection is going to be about. Once he makes a prediction, ask what clues in the story helped him make his prediction. Check his logic in developing predictions. Has he read the text carefully so a logical prediction is made? Again, tell him to read to a certain point and check his prediction. When he finishes, let him discuss his prediction in relation to what happened in the selection. Repeat this process until your child finishes reading the entire selection.

For a very short selection, you may ask for only one prediction, and your child will read the entire text. For a longer selection, you may break up the reading by asking your child to stop at an exciting part of the story and make a second prediction of how the story may end. Use your own judgment about the number of pages your child should read before the discussion. Children who experience comprehension difficulties should read shorter segments. But too many stops within a story can ruin your child's enjoyment for reading. After you and your child try this activity a few times, you'll be able to estimate the number of necessary stops for developing your child's comprehension. A helpful hint: Choose stories that have a good plot. This seems to make the DRTA approach work better.

5. Most children love cartoons. Use them to develop sequencing skills in reading. Cut out cartoon strips from the newspaper and separate the cartoon frames. Put a number on the back of each cartoon frame to identify the correct sequence. Place each cartoon strip in an envelope. For convenience, store the envelopes in a recipe file. Help your child to sequence by telling him to spread out and read all the frames to that cartoon and then put them in order. Reading all the frames before sequencing helps develop the main topic and sequencing is easier. Your child can check his sequence by turning the cartoon frames over and checking the numerical order.

6. Many children love the paperback series entitled "Choose Your Own Adventure" published by Bantam Books. Each book is an adventure asking the reader to make choices at different points within the book. There are several choices at each point. Each choice leads the reader to experience a new adventure. To check your child's understanding, discuss the sequence of the story events.

7. Children, by nature, are curious about the world around them. They want to know: Where do babies come from? Why does feeling chilly cause goose bumps? What causes the chain reaction in falling dominoes? These are interesting questions, and often the answers can be found in books.

    Write out the questions your child has been asking. Together, you and your child can look up books in the subject index of the card catalog at the library or use other reference books such as atlases and encyclopedias. After the two of you have found the right source, silently read the passage and have your child tell you the answer to his question. He may need guidance with his explanation. Or he may need guidance to identify the part or parts of the passage that provide answers to his questions. Be patient, this is not an easy task. But the reward is great. Your child learns that books can provide information and solve problems.

8. If your child enjoys problem and solution reading, try *The Science Book* by Sara Stein. It is written for children who love discovering answers to their questions about animals, insects, plants, human beings, electricity, et cetera. Your child investigates and experiments. But to do so, he must first read and understand the author's directions and discussions. Many short topics are discussed so you can help guide your child's understanding in a relatively short time. One example from Stein's book is the investigation of how popcorn is grown. Through reading, using illustrations, and perhaps even planting popcorn, your child can develop an understanding of the way popcorn grows and develops. Other books like Stein's can be found in your library.

9. Cut out several short articles from magazines. Separate the title from the article. Mix up the articles and the titles. Ask your child to match the correct title with the article. Make sure you select articles that are interesting and that can be read fairly easily.

10. Hobbies are good ways to get children reading. Help your child select books on his hobbies. You might help him design a project directly relating to his interests. For example, if your child is in-

terested in stamp collecting, suggest reading some stamp collecting books and making a manual for his own use.

11. Riddles can be an enjoyable way to develop comprehension skill. Select some riddle books and take turns by reading riddles to each other and try to solve the riddle. You may like to start with these riddle books:

> *Riddles, Riddles, Riddles* selected by Joseph Leeming. New York: Franklin Watts, Inc. 1953.
>
> *A Book of Puzzlements* by Herbert Kohl. New York: Schocken Books, 1981.
>
> *The Nonsense Book* collected by Duncan Enrich. New York: Four Winds Press, 1970.
>
> *Fiddle With a Riddle* by Joanne E. Bernstein. New York: E.P. Dutton, 1979.

12. To play the popular fantasy game "Dungeons and Dragons," children need to read and apply the information learned from the various game books. Reading these books helps game players make wise decisions so they can win the game. To enhance your child's learning, read the books with him and play the game together. *Dungeons and Dragons* books are written by Gary Gyax for TSR Games.

Another fantasy game book, *Adventures in High Fantasy,* has been written by Jeffrey C. Dillow. These high fantasy games are quite different from the typical box games like Monopoly. They involve reading, thinking, and imagining and serve as good monitors for improved reading skills.

Comprehension is improved by continually reading, thinking, and applying what you have learned from text. One learns to become an expert pianist by playing the piano. The same is true for reading. You become a skilled reader by constantly reading. The best advice I can give parents is to encourage their children to read. By reading often, your child is practicing the skills and concepts developed in school and home. Growth and skill in reading will be the end result.

Vocabulary

Of all the reading skills that affect comprehension, vocabulary is considered the most important. To discuss or read about any specialized topic, technical vocabulary has to be used. Try to understand the following passage without the vocabulary knowledge of computers.

> PAR estimates the parameters of a nonlinear function by least squares using a pseudo-Gauss-Newton algorithm (Ralston and Jennrich, 1977). PAR is appropriate for a wide variety of functions that are not linear in the parameters, and for which derivatives are difficult to specify or costly to compute. The nonlinear function must be specified by FORTRAN statements; the derivatives are *not* specified.

> (SPSS: *Statistical Package for the Social Sciences* by N. Nie, D.H. Bent, and C.H. Hull. New York: McGraw Hill, 1970. Trademark SPSS Inc., Chicago, Illinois.)

As you read the passage, you probably found it more and more difficult to understand because you didn't know the words. Vocabulary knowledge is crucial to comprehension. Without it, you can't apply what is read. This important skill can be developed through personal experiences, direct instruction, and incidental learning.

The best way to develop vocabulary is through personal experiences. A child learns the meanings of words by experiencing places, things, and events. For example, take your child to the planetarium and talk about the different constellations you view together. Continue the discussion at home by reading and discussing books about planets and stars. Even the simplest everyday event, such as trying a new food or repairing something in your house, can provide your child with new vocabulary.

In school, your child also receives direct vocabulary instruction. Typically, teachers provide explanations and discussions about new words. They teach children to use context to figure out unknown words. Meanings of roots, prefixes, and suffixes are also taught. Dictionary instruction is given as well as synonyms (words with similar meanings), antonyms (words with opposite meanings), and multiple meanings of words.

Your child also develops vocabulary knowledge incidentally. Leisure-time reading increases vocabulary. Listening and talking to others can be another source of learning new vocabulary.

As a parent you can increase your child's vocabulary with the following activities:

1. Visit places and take part in activities. Discuss the specialized vocabulary of the particular place and event. Personal experiences can be a stimulus for improving your child's reading skill.

2. Password is an enjoyable game for the entire family. To play, write a different word on separate pieces of paper and place words in an empty box. Two teams of at least two players each are needed to play. Players from each team try to guess the selected word when given one-word clues from their respective team members. Play begins when team one selects a word from the box and provides a single-word clue to its team member. Only one response is permitted. If the response is correct on the first attempt, the team receives 10 points. If the response is incorrect, the second team is permitted to give a new one-word clue. If the second team's member makes a correct response, the team receives nine points. If incorrect, the first team resumes play. Turns alternate, with each succeeding guess earning one less point. Once a word is guessed correctly, another word is selected. Team two begins the second round. By playing Password,

you will find your children learning antonyms and synonyms and increasing their word power and reading power.

3. Scrabble is another game that can be enjoyed by the entire family. For the younger child, you may want to start with the less complicated Scrabble for Juniors. Boggle, another word game, can also serve as an introductory game to Scrabble. All these games not only help increase your child's word power, but are also enjoyable leisure-time activities.

4. Another vocabulary game is Categories. Any number of people can play. The game consists of choosing five unrelated categories, such as transportation, color, tools, fruit, and vegetables. Write these on the top of a piece of paper. Choose any word and write it vertically on the left side of the paper. Allow three minutes for play. Write the most words appropriate to the category that starts with the same letter found in the left-hand column. An example of a completed game sheet is provided below.

	tools	clothes	transportation	fruit	vegetables
d		dress			
a	ax			apple	artichoke
r		raincoat			radish
t			taxi	tangerine	
s	saw	shoes	skates	strawberry	

After the game is completed, each player explains why the words belong to each category. A dictionary can be used to check accuracy. The player who has written the most correct words wins the game.

5. If your child enjoys drawing, select words he can draw, then label the drawing as in the example below.

Mallard

Or select words whose meaning your child can illustrate as in this example:

6. Try to get your child hooked on crossword puzzles. There are children's crosswords published by Dell that can be found in most bookstores. The author, Herb Kohl, suggests some interesting word puzzles for children in *A Book of Puzzlements*.

7. Children love the appealing Mad Libs which are pads of paper with short, interesting selections. Mad Libs, written by Rober Price and Leonard Stein, are published by Price, Stein, and Sloan. In a Mad Lib, the child supplies words for the blanks within the passage. The selected words must make logical sense as well as match the appropriate part of speech identified in the passage. Your child may enjoy comparing his completed Mad Libs with others. More than one word can be correct. You may even want to try writing your own uncompleted Mad Libs or have your child write some for you.

8. The game Dictionary can be an enjoyable experience for the entire family. A dictionary, pencil, and paper are needed for this game. Player one identifies a word that is usually unique and unknown by the players. Each player writes a definition for the selected word. Player one writes the dictionary definition. All definitions are placed in a box and read aloud by player one. Each player selects a definition he believes to be the correct one for the selected word. After each player has selected a definition, the correct one is read. Those who have selected the appropriate definition receive one point. Play continues in the same manner with player two selecting another word, and each player writing a definition. At the end of a complete round, each player tallies up the points earned. The player with the greatest number of points wins the game.

Selecting Books

A key to reading is selecting appropriate books that match your child's present reading abilities and interests. A book that is too difficult can only frustrate your child and cause him to stop reading it. A book that is too easy can reinforce what he knows about the world, but it also can lack sparkle and challenge. (An easy book is appropriate when your child is totally on his own, receiving no assistance from you.) The most appropriate level at which you and your child can work together is labeled the "instructional level."

This is how you can identify your child's instructional level: Select a book and ask him to read aloud approximately 100 words. If he makes four or five mistakes that change the passage meaning, yet understands 75 percent of what is read, then the book is at your child's instructional level. If he makes more than five errors altering the passage meaning and does not really understand what is read, then the book is too difficult and is at your child's frustration level. When your child makes less than two meaningful mistakes and has understood the passage well, then the book is at your child's independent level. Use this chart to help identify your child's reading levels.

Reading Level	Meaningful Errors in Oral Reading	Comprehension of Passage
Independent	1−2	95%
Instructional	4−5	75%
Frustration	more than 5	50%

(Developed by Emmett Betts)

You may want your child to read two or three passages at different places in the book to make sure the book is at the appropriate reading level. Comprehending the passage is important, so check your child's understanding by asking ten questions. As you work with your child, try to have him read books at his instructional level. Avoid books at the frustration level, since meaningful learning will not take place.

Besides matching the appropriate text with your child's reading ability, you need to consider his interests. Your child will enjoy and learn more if he is interested and motivated. Choosing books he dislikes will only be an uphill battle and may cause your child to respond negatively as well as withdraw from learning.

Reading to Learn

By the time your child reaches the middle grades (4-8), he is expected to know *how* to read. Now his task is to focus on developing skills to obtain information from reading. Reading to learn is a major factor in science and social studies. During the middle-grade years, children spend a larger portion of their school day learning about science and social studies. Reading science and social studies is quite a different task than reading a fictitious story. Your child must know some facts and concepts to learn effectively from textbooks. Not only is he faced with reading about facts, but the vocabulary and the writing style are quite different from story writing. The vocabulary is technical and specific to the subject. For example, children know what the word "chain" means but often don't know the meaning of "food chain." The writing style in science and social studies tends to be pattern-like. For example, an author may use a problem-solving pattern to explain a concept.

Knowing So You Can Learn More

Science and social studies can be made easy for your child if he already knows something about the topic to be studied. The child who has grown his own vegetable and flower garden has acquired some valuable information to apply when reading a textbook chapter on plants. The child whose hobby is reading books on gliders, helicopters, jets, and spacecraft is better prepared to understand textbook chapters on flight and space. The key elements for textbook learning are reading and doing activities related to topics studied in science and social studies. Let's discuss a few practical suggestions for helping your child learn more from textbooks.

1. Look through your child's textbooks and identify the topics to be studied in social studies and science. Talk to your child's teacher and find out when each topic will be studied. Use this information to select library books on the topics your child is studying at school. If your child knows little about the topic, select books that are rather easy to read. Select more challenging books if he is familiar with the topic. Encourage your child to select some interesting and motivating books on each topic. Read and discuss the information you both learn. This is a good opportunity to use the "Request" technique that was described earlier in this chapter.

2. Many times teachers don't have the time for activities or experiments to help children better understand new concepts. As a parent, this gives you the perfect opportunity to do some of the suggested activities and experiments in your child's textbook. Most of these activities don't require specialized or expensive equipment. Many use household items. Do the activities pertaining to the topic your child is presently studying in school. As you do the activity, discuss what is happening.

3. Read the science and social studies chapters your child is studying at school. Sit down with your child and discuss the facts and concepts presented in these chapters. Review these concepts at different times so your child has several opportunities to learn them.

4. Teachers are limited to the number of field trips they can plan. But these are the experiences in which children can learn a great deal. Consider the topics being studied in school and choose places that can enrich your child's learning. If your child is studying planets and the universe, make a trip to the planetarium. If industry and manufacturing is a social studies topic, contact local companies about guided tours. First-hand experiences provide your child with a wealth of information as well as being very enjoyable. And such trips are not expensive!

Technical Vocabulary — Important or Not?

As with comprehension of all written materials, vocabulary plays a major role in subject area textbooks. Your child needs to develop the specific technical vocabulary to understand the content of science and social studies. Technical vocabulary is best learned while a child is reading, experimenting, and observing this area of science and social studies. Learning endless lists of words without continually reading and discussing these words is not beneficial. Your child doesn't see the purpose for learning these words and, as a result, may lack motivation and commitment for increasing his vocabulary.

To increase your child's knowledge of technical vocabulary, try the following activities, coordinating them with topics your child is reading and discussing in school.

1. Browse through the textbook chapters your child is currently studying at school. Select technical words important to the contents of the chapter. Try to incorporate these words in daily conversations with your child.

2. Encourage your child to use a dictionary or glossary to correctly pronounce words and understand the meaning used in context. The key to using the dictionary effectively is to read the entire sentence containing the unknown word. Use the context to provide meaning clues. Now refer to the dictionary to choose the appropriate definition. Reread the sentence, checking the accuracy of the definition selected.

3. Use the vocabulary from a chapter your child is currently studying. Cut 1" by 2" cards so a technical word can be written on each card. Cut 1" by 5" cards to write the corresponding definition of each technical word. Mix up the word cards. Now mix up the definition cards. Ask your child to correctly match the word with its definition.

4. Play the game Password with the technical vocabulary from two or three textbook chapters your child has studied. This can be a good vocabulary review.

5. Many children like crossword puzzles. Design your own, using the technical vocabulary from a chapter in the textbook your child is currently reading in school.

6. The importance of doing activities and experiments was mentioned earlier in this chapter. As you and your child engage in science and social studies activities, use the technical vocabulary found in his textbook.

7. The value of visiting places related to science and social studies was also discussed earlier. Try to use the technical vocabulary while visiting places related to the topics under study.

8. Use your child's textbooks to show him how to use context to understand new words. Many textbooks have the word defined within the sentence. Authors also use synonyms to provide understanding for a new word. Summary sentences sometimes are used to develop a new word's meaning. Help your child to use these clues to easily increase his vocabulary.

9. Teach your child to use root words, prefixes, and suffixes to unlock word meanings. Science and social studies contain a number of root words. For example, the roots "ology" and "scope" are used in many areas of science. Focusing on common roots provides your child with an invaluable tool for learning new words. (A list of common roots can be found on page 251.)

The suggested vocabulary activities should increase your child's word power. Make these experiences interesting and enjoyable, not drudgery. Your child will learn more when he is motivated and interested.

Using Writing Style to Increase Learning

As your child moves from fiction to textbook reading, he'll notice some changes. The predictable story with a beginning, middle, and end is no longer characteristic. Rather, science and social studies textbooks contain a variety of writing patterns emphasizing information to be learned. Your child's task is to become familiar with the common writing patterns so he can identify this important information.

One common writing style your child will read in textbooks is a question-answer pattern. A question is posed followed by the answer. This pattern can be quite simple if the question is directly stated and followed by a specific answer. Other times, the question is stated but only clues are given to answer the question. Now your child has to piece together the clues and add his knowledge to reach an answer. This kind of writing pattern adds the dimension of problem-solving. It can be a bit more challenging for your child. Let's take a look at an example of a question-answer pattern from a sixth-grade science textbook.

Where Do You Get All Your Energy?

Ecosystems run on energy. It takes energy for plants and animals to grow and reproduce. It takes energy to walk and see and make sounds. It takes energy to keep from freezing on a cold day.

Ecosystems depend on the sun for their energy. Solar energy can take several forms.

One form is heat. Sunlight warms up plants and animals and their environments.

Green plants make another use of sunlight. They trap light energy and use it to make food. Animals make use of this form of solar energy when they eat plants or other animals that have eaten plants. All the eating interactions make up food webs. Some of the food builds body parts. The rest supplies energy for the animals' activities.

A third form of solar energy is stored in fuels such as coal, oil, natural gas, and firewood. The energy in these materials is released when they burn. These fuels all come from living things. Coal, oil, and natural gas come from living things that died millions of years ago.)

(Berger/Berkheimer/Neuberger/Lewis: HOUGHTON MIFFLIN SCIENCE, Copyright ©1979 Houghton Mifflin Company. Used with permission.)

What is nice about this textbook is the clear presentation of the writing pattern! The question is in boldface type and serves as a chapter heading. The textbook format cues your child about what is to be learned, but, at the same time, this textbook challenges your child's thinking. The answer isn't spelled out. Your child must identify the clues, piece them together, and add his personal experiences to answer the question.

How can you help your child learn the important information from this writing pattern? First, check to see if any of your child's textbooks use this pattern. If so, select those sections using the question-answer pattern. If possible, select those sections your child is currently reading in school. The reading will be more relevant and motivating. The technique for reading question-answer patterns is to read for the purpose of answering the stated question. Explain to your child that when this pattern is used, the author is pointing out the significance of the question and answer and is alerting the reader to important information. To learn and remember this information, tell your child to read for the purpose of answering the question. After reading, invite your child to explain the answer in his own words. Practice this technique with several different chapter passages that contain the question-answer pattern. When your child reads on his own, suggest he recite the answer aloud. Then you reread the section to check his recitation. Or your child may want to use a tape recorder to check his recitation. Another alternative: he may find it helpful to write the question and answer in his own words. His written notes can help him study for tests.

A second common pattern is topic development. Textbooks often develop a topic over several paragraphs that discuss important facts and ideas. Usually a heading is used to identify the topic. It is one of the simpler patterns to read, but selecting important information tends to be difficult. Which fact or idea is significant? It isn't always clear and many times depends on what your child's teacher emphasizes. Let's take a look at a typical example from a sixth-grade social studies textbook.

The Berlin Wall

Today another wall stands as a famous boundary marker, but with an important difference. The purpose of this wall is not to keep invaders out but to keep people from leaving the nation! This wall is known as the Berlin Wall. It was built by the government of East Germany.

In 1945, at the end of World War II, the winning Allies divided Germany into different parts. These parts were called zones of occupation. Three nations—the United States, France, and Great Britain—kept troops in the western zones. The Soviet Union stationed troops in the central zone. Find these zones on the map on this page. The part of Germany nearest to Poland was given to Poland. It has been part of Poland ever since.

In 1949 the three western zones were joined to form West Germany, a republic with its capital in Bonn. The Soviet zone, with a Communist form of government, became East Germany.

Berlin, the old German capital city, is in East Germany. However, Berlin itself was divided into east and west zones. East Berlin became the capital of East Germany.

At first, people could move freely from East Germany to West Germany. Thousands of East Berliners traveled every day between their homes in East Berlin and their jobs in West Berlin. But many never returned home. They simply stayed in West Berlin or moved to parts of West Germany. About three million people left East Germany. Many were trained and educated people.

East German officials closed the borders in August 1961. Then they built a wall thirty miles long through Berlin. Guards with dogs and searchlights patrol the wall. All the houses along the East Berlin side of the wall have been emptied. Now no one can move from East Berlin to West Berlin without permission. But people still try to escape.

(From THE WORLD: LIVING IN OUR WORLD by Paul F. Brandwein and Nancy W. Bauer, copyright ©1980 by Harcourt Brace Jovanovich, Inc. Reprinted by permission of the publisher.)

Notice there are many facts given about the Berlin Wall, and not all of these facts are important. How can you help your child learn the important points and not get buried in trivia? The following technique can help solve this problem. Choose sections from your child's textbook that use a topic development pattern. Show your child how headings alert the reader to the type of writing pattern as in the example "The Berlin Wall." For his first experience with a topic development pattern, read the section aloud. Together decide which facts are important. Your discussion of important versus non-important facts will prepare him for reading a topic development pattern independently. Note the important points on a sheet of paper. Once the reading is completed, the notes will help your child compose a summary. The summary can be oral or written. Encourage him to use this technique while reading independently.

Your child will also need to become familiar with the comparison-contrast pattern. In this pattern, important information is developed by identifying likenesses and differences among objects and events. In some textbooks, authors literally state the relationships. In others, authors expect your child to observe and develop his own comparisons. Let's examine a fifth-grade science textbook that expects your child to discover likenesses and differences between plant and animal cells.

Looking at Cells

Observe some plant and animal cells. Find out how they are alike and different.

First, get some cells to look at. Here is how to get some different plant cells.

Get a wedge cut from a fresh onion. Remove one layer. Peel off some of the thin skin on the layer. Picture A shows how. Place a small piece of the onion skin on a glass slide.

Your teacher may give you a special water plant with tiny leaves. Put a leaf on a slide.

Now get some animal cells.

Gently scrape the inside of your cheek with the flat end of a toothpick. This will remove some mouth cells. Rub the moist toothpick on a glass slide as shown in picture B. This will put some mouth cells on the slide.

Next, prepare your slides for observation. Add a drop of iodine to stain the onion and mouth cells. Picture C shows how. This makes the cells easier to see. Add a drop of water to the leaf. Then cover each slide with a cover slip, as shown in picture D. Look at each slide through a microscope.

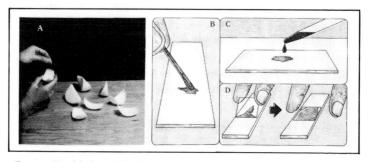

In this example, your child has to conduct the experiment and make the observations to develop comparisons and contrasts. In other textbooks, the author identifies the specific comparisons and contrasts to be learned. Key phrases are often used to alert the reader to a comparison or contrast. For example, these phrases are often used: "the same characteristics describe," "in contrast," "in comparison," et cetera. Most of these phrases appear at the beginning or ending of a sentence.

Your child can gather information from this pattern by using a chart method. Select passages from your child's textbooks using a comparison-contrast pattern. Design a chart like the one below. Tell your child to read the passage that identifies the objects or events being compared. As your child notes a likeness or difference, he places the information in the appropriate chart column. He continues until the passage has been completely read. The chart is a good tool for reviewing and studying for a test.

Likenesses	Differences

108

Sequencing is another common pattern found in textbooks. The author uses this pattern to identify and explain the steps in a process or experiment. Here is a typical example of a sequencing pattern appearing in a fifth-grade science textbook. The child has to follow the labeled steps closely to construct the pinwheel.

Model A Pinwheel

Motion in one direction can cause motion in another direction. In the next few lessons you will study this idea. You will make and use pinwheels to help you.

Make the Model A pinwheel. Your teacher will give you a paper pattern. Write your name on the largest pattern piece. Color the pattern pieces red. Follow steps a through h to make your pinwheel.

Step a. Cut along the solid lines of all of the Model A pattern pieces.

Step b. Stick a pin through each dot to make holes.

Step c. Roll the shaft *loosely* around a pencil. Tape the end together. Bend back the tabs along the dotted lines, as shown in the picture below. Take the shaft off the pencil.

Step d. Bring the corners of the pinwheel together. All of the holes you made should meet at the center hole.

Step e. Put a long pin through all of the holes in the pinwheel. Then put the pin through the shaft and through the hole in the base.

Caution
Be careful. The pin is very sharp.

Step f. Stick the pin in your pencil eraser.

Step g. Glue one set of shaft tabs to the back of the pinwheel.

Step h. Glue the other set of tabs to the base. Your pinwheel should look like this.

(Berger/Berkheimer/Neuberger/Lewis: HOUGHTON MIFFLIN SCIENCE, Copyright ©1979 Houghton Mifflin Company. Used with permission.)

To learn information from a sequential pattern, it is advantageous for your child first to read the section at a moderate rate. This reading rate helps your child develop a mind set for the task to be completed. A slower, second reading should follow to discover the details and sequence of the task. Many times a picture accompanies a sequential pattern. Your child should refer to the picture as well as the passage to develop understanding. The best way to check sequential pattern comprehension is to encourage your child to do the task suggested in his textbook. Compare his outcome with the one in the textbook. If the outcome is different, your child knows he didn't follow the text closely enough. The task can then be attempted again. The repetition can help your child see where he made an error.

How to Read Text Effectively

Reading textbooks, in general, can be a difficult task for children. Children often sit down and begin to read textbooks just as they have read stories. They don't realize that there is a preparation or previewing task so learning is made easier. To get the most out of reading, your child needs to think about what will be presented in the text and relate it to what he knows about the topic. To do this, teach your child how to preview a textbook chapter. Use this step-by-step approach:

First, read the title. It is the first clue to the main idea of the chapter or text. Next, read the introduction and/or the summary to get an overall view of the concepts to be learned in the chapter.

Now your child is ready to begin step two. In this step, your child previews some of the minor concepts and important details. He can begin by reading the main headings and subheadings. Suggest he also spend some time looking at italicized words within the body of the chapter. If he is unfamiliar with the word, read the sentence containing the italicized word to gain a better understanding. Or suggest he use the glossary or dictionary to acquire word meaning. If the chapter contains illustrations, graphs, maps, etc., recommend he spend time previewing these pictorial devices. Most times a picture can say 1,000 words. Your child can remember information as well as become more involved in reading when textbooks include graphs and other types of illustrations.

The last step requires your child to formulate some questions before he begins reading. The following prereading questions would be quite appropriate: What is this chapter going to be about? What seems to be the important concepts? Once your child develops a question, suggest he predict its answer. Now he has a purpose for reading. As he reads, he can think about the accuracy of his predicted answer.

These steps don't take long, and they can help your child read and comprehend at a faster rate. After reading the chapter, your child should compare his prediction to the information he learned from reading. Invite him to discuss the major concepts he has learned. Discuss the concepts with him. Reread any parts of the chapter that seem confusing to your child. Encourage him to use previewing when he reads independently. Suggest he continue to tell or write about the concepts he has learned. He can check his own comprehension by reviewing and rereading parts of the chapter.

A Note about Notes

Notetaking is a beneficial skill. It can help children better remember what was read as well as increase their test scores. Too often children think notetaking is a laborious, useless task. It seems to be only "busy work." The notetaking ideas suggested here try to avoid this stereotype. They are rather quick, effortless ways to improve learning. You will find your middle schooler easily adopting these notetaking techniques.

Good notetaking requires your child to think and make

decisions about important ideas. Good notetaking doesn't follow a prescribed model. There is no one best way to take notes. Notetaking models can be provided, but your child has to choose and adjust the model to best suit his needs.

In the first model, your child should use a stenographer's notebook to record his notes. To begin, preview the chapter and identify what topics will be presented. If the chapter is divided in sections, read the first subheading and turn it into a question or questions. Write a short version of each question in the left-hand column of the steno pad. Now read the entire section looking for the answer. In the right-hand column, write phrases to answer the question. Let's look at an example of this kind of notetaking.

| What are carpetbaggers? | Northern Republicans who were supposedly taking advantage of blacks and bad conditions in South |
| What are scalawags? | White southerners who became Republicans |

Repeat this process with each subheading. After the chapter is read, your child can easily use these notes to study for a test. Cover the right-hand answer column and read the question. Then check the answer by reading the right-hand column.

A second notetaking technique uses 8½x11 notebook paper. If your child's textbook uses subheadings, this second technique is helpful. As your child comes to a chapter subheading, he should read it and write down the main topic in the left-hand margin. Next, your child reads the section to identify the major points. After the section is read, your child writes the main points in the right-hand section of the paper. An example of this notetaking model is found on the next page.

| Navigation Acts | 1. Colonies could only sell their raw materials to Mother England. |
| | 2. England manufactured products with these raw materials and sold to colonies for a large profit. |

Developing Flexibility of Reading Rate

Should your child read all types of material at the same rate? The answer to this question is definitely no. Your child needs to read various types of materials at different rates. In other words, his reading rate needs to be flexible. When your child reads textbooks or any other factual material, he should read it at a comfortable but smooth rate. A high level of comprehension should be maintained. If he reads too slowly, he will be unable to comprehend the author's ideas. However, reading technical material at a rapid rate is not recommended. The content and vocabulary are probably unfamiliar to your child. Reading stories or other recreational reading is the time for your child to read at a more rapid rate. The content and vocabulary are probably familiar, so a faster reading pace will not cause poor comprehension.

But, generally, children don't change their reading rate when reading different types of materials. They not only read all materials at the same rate, but they read too slowly. During the middle grades, I have found that children feel they need to read every word on the page to comprehend the author's message. You'll often see children reading silently and moving their lips. What they are doing is reading orally in their heads! Lip movement or subvocalization promotes slow deliberate reading and tends to hinder comprehension.

How can you, as a parent, help your child achieve flexibility in reading rate? First of all, it is unnecessary to read *all* the words on a page no matter what kind of material is being read. Encourage your child to read only the important words in a sentence and disregard the unimportant ones. The function words, such as "the," "this," "a," "that," "to," "up," etc., are not vital to comprehension, so skip over them. However, nouns, verbs, adjectives, and adverbs are very necessary for comprehension, and these are the words to be read.

Second, tell your child to read in phrases with his eyes, not with his lips. Reading in phrases can be accomplished by looking for meaningful phrases within a sentence. For example, read the adjective and noun together and then focus on the verb and adverb. Look at the sentence below. Which words should your child read?

The pretty bird flew gracefully in the air.

"Pretty bird" should be read together as well as "flew gracefully." These are the words that develop sentence meaning.

Use the following technique to develop your child's ability to read in phrases. Type a short story and draw arcs under the parts of the sentence that he should be reading, such as an arc under the adjective and noun. Let him try reading only those parts that are marked and check his comprehension. At first, he will feel uncomfortable with not reading every word on the page. But with practice, your child will see how his silent reading will improve. Type out a few short stories and let him make the arcs under those phrases he thinks he should be reading. Encourage him to practice phrase reading while reading for pleasure; then try it with textbook reading.

Another technique for increasing your child's reading rate is employing three- to five-minute timings. Choose short articles from magazines like *Geographic World, Cobblestone,* et cetera. Ask a question prior to reading. Remind your child to read in phrases. For each silent reading timing, record the number of words per minute he reads. Your youngster can readily see his growth, or lack of it, each time he completes a timing. If his rate becomes slower, discuss the possible reasons for this. Was the topic unfamiliar? Was he not reading in phrases? Did he have to slow down due to unknown words? Was he paying attention to the information in the story? These and other questions can help your child analyze his changes in reading rate. After each timing, ask questions or discuss what was read. Help your child understand that comprehension, not reading speed, is the most important element of reading.

Social and Emotional Growth and Its Effect on Learning

A child begins the long road of adolescence around the age of eleven. It is during adolescence that your child needs to be self-confident. Feeling good about himself, both in and out of school, can help him through the uncertainties and changes that occur during adolescence. At this time parents need to be particularly helpful and to acknowledge and appreciate their child's efforts. Even the smallest improvement in grades on a report card should be noticed and commended. Positive reinforcement during this age can work wonders!

It is during this time that the adolescent struggles with feelings of inferiority. Consequently, if your child has any academic weaknesses, he is likely to avoid these weak areas and concentrate on areas in which he is strong. Pushing your child to meet his weakness head on may not be the answer. For example, if your youngster is having difficulties with reading comprehension, forcing him to read books too difficult for him is clearly not the best solution. Making your child feel less than confident about his reading abilities is not motivational. In fact, it may encourage him to avoid books totally. It is better to provide your child with books that are easy to read and are specifically directed to his interests and hobbies. When you show your child that you believe he can do well and will succeed, you will more likely see a change in school achievement.

During this period, adolescents are keenly aware of and sensitive to peers' thoughts and feelings. Peer pressure is strong, and peer approval can affect your child's actions and performance in school. For example, if it is acceptable to receive good grades, then your child will probably work toward getting good marks. If good grades are not revered, then your child's grades may suffer. How can parents counteract the latter problem? From the time he enters school, you can show interest in his learning. Praising and rewarding his efforts from early on is the key. Develop your child's self-confidence so he overcomes the great need for peer approval. Parents can also put peer pressure and approval into proper perspective by giving him the opportunity to show his strengths and importance to the family. By accepting and recognizing your child as a worthwhile person, you can do much to diminish the power of peers.

The adolescent is also seeking independence, and this search creates positive and negative consequences. For example, you may want to help him be a better student, but he may reject your assistance and want to succeed on his own. One way to deal with such independence is to ask him to provide suggestions for improving his grades. Eliciting his help and direction may be the beginning step in developing a good working relationship, and the end result may be better grades.

The adolescent also has a need to be introspective and to examine his personal values, ideas, and identity. Frequently, the adolescent not only thinks about what he should do but also discusses it with himself. Parents can help in their child's self-clarification by supplying fiction novels dealing with adolescent problems and conflicts, such as honesty, divorce, illness, personal appearance, et cetera. Books can provide a means for self-understanding and insight into common problems facing today's adolescent. Many authors write about adolescent conflicts and dilemmas. A listing of such books can be found in these library resources:

Carlson, G.R. *Books and the Teen-Age Reader.* New York: Harper & Row, 1967.

Tway, E. (Ed.) *Reading Ladders for Human Relations.* Urbana, Il.: National Council of Teachers of English, 1981.

Walker, J.L. *A Booklist for Junior High Students.* Urbana, IL: National Council of Teachers of English, 1975.

The Organizational Structure of Schools

What Happens in School

When your child enters the middle grades, the organization of the school day changes gradually over the next four years. By the time your child reaches eighth grade, he will most likely have a different teacher for each subject area. Each of these teachers will probably be a specialist in the subject area being taught. Your child will also experience changing classes for each subject. There will probably be different students in each of his classes. Changing classes and experiencing different teachers and classmates are great changes for the adolescent. Adjustment may be slow. In the beginning months, grades may be negatively affected. With time and your support, your child will adjust.

One of the changes during the middle grades is that reading may no longer be separately taught but may be part of the language arts program in which your child receives instruction in reading, spelling, handwriting, speaking, listening, and writing. There are probably separate books for English, spelling, and reading. The reading text is most likely a continuation of the same basal series begun in kindergarten or first grade. This same series may be continued until the end of eighth grade. However, in some schools, parents may find their seventh- and eighth-grader encountering a literature text and novels rather than the basal reader.

It is also during the middle grades that language arts teachers spend much instructional time developing literary elements such as characterization, plot, figurative language, et cetera. More intense writing assignments focus on literature read for class. This is also a time when study skills receive instructional priority. Learning how to use the library for finding information and writing reports are important areas developed during the middle grades. By the end of the middle grades, your child is expected to know how to read, how to acquire information from reading, and how to communicate information. As a parent, make sure your child is proficient in each of the above areas. If he is not, then ask for his teachers' suggestions for gaining these skills. The activities provided in this book can develop all three of these skills.

Homework

Each school has a different philosophy toward homework. Although drill and repetition is a part of the learning process, don't assume that repetition helps your child to organize, sequence, and finish a task more efficiently. Recent research indicates that children must be taught how to organize and sequence the task. Simply doing it many times is not enough. Homework in itself does not necessarily teach all skills. Two hours of homework each night actually proves nothing about the quality of the educational program. Homework should help your child reinforce and apply all that has been learned in school. It should not end up being "busy work."

Homework time can be a period of conflict for parents and child. Parents often ask a child if the homework is finished. The child responds, "Yes" and heads out the door to be with friends. It is only at 10:30 at night, or through a parent-teacher conference, that you discover your child "forgot" about an assignment or is not doing assigned work. If these problems occur, here is a suggestion. Set aside a specific hour each day for quiet time. During this hour, your child is to read or do any of his school assignments. TV and other distractions should be eliminated. It is advantageous if your child has his own desk, bookshelves, and a comfortable chair for reading. If 7:30 — 8:30 each night must be a quiet time at his desk, then your child will read or do his assignments. The problem and the daily battles will lessen because the question is not "Do you have any homework?" but "What will you work on tonight?"

Continual Renewal of the Parent-Teacher Partnership

Communication between parent and teacher is a vital part of ensuring your child's success in school. Visits to the school can be important for gathering information about what occurs in the classroom. Conferring with your child's teacher should not occur in the morning five minutes before school begins. The teacher is rushed, and your child's classmates are usually within listening distance. Conferences should take place when there is time and privacy to discuss your child's progress. In the beginning school years, when your child has one teacher, contact can be made on a fairly regular basis. As your child begins to have several teachers, the task of communication becomes more difficult. In some schools, children have more than one teacher as early as grade four. If there is more than one subject area teacher, conferences are even more important. This is particularly true if your child is going through a troublesome or stressful period.

Before contacting the school, tell your child you're interested in talking to his teacher(s). Try to receive his support and approval. As the parent of an adolescent, you must be careful about visiting school and calling teachers. During this age, adolescents are developing their own identity and do not appreciate adult interference. Thus, if school-related problems occur, your first step is to discuss the matter with your child. If the problem needs school involvement, your next step is to contact the school and ask for a conference. Probably the most successful conferences at this age include your child. The result is often a welcome solution to problems because your child is involved in the process of solving them.

Additional Suggestions for Parents

1. Continue to expand your child's vocabulary. Discuss specific vocabulary used during conversations. Do not hesitate to ask your child if he knows the meaning of a word. Vocabulary is the

basis for reading improvement. Some of the following ideas may enhance discussions and increase your child's vocabulary:
- double meanings (The boy felt *blue* when the aunt left the *blue* boat.)
- synonyms – same meaning of words (rapid, quick)
- homonyms – same sound spelled differently (flower, flour)
- figurative language and idiomatic expressions (Darkness fell over the sky. The clouds are soft like pillows.)

2. Develop visual imagery. In this world of vast exposure to media children need not rely on their own ability to create images in their minds. Encourage your child to create images from reading interesting stories. He may enjoy drawing what he has read. Or he may enjoy discussing the images he developed in his mind. You may want to ask questions to develop these images. For example, if a passage is particularly exciting, ask what the action looks like, how a person looks, and what the scenery is like.

3. Subscribe to magazines that your child finds interesting. The following list can provide you with initial choices:

Penny Power
Penny Power Magazine
256 Washington Street
Mount Vernon, NY 10550

National Wildlife
1412 16th Street, NW
Washington DC 20036

Dynamite
730 Broadway
New York, NY 10003

Odyssey
Astro Media Corp.
625 E. St. Paul Ave.
P.O. Box 92788
Milwaukee, WI 53202

Sport
Sport Magazine
Box 5014
Lake Geneva, WI 53147

Dragon
Dragon Publishing
P.O. Box 110
Lake Geneva, WI 53147

Teen
Teen Magazine
6725 Sunset Blvd.
P.O. Box 3297
Los Angeles, CA 90028

4. Buy books for your child that encourage reading and making crafts or objects. An example is *Carpentry for Children* by Lester Walker. In this book, children read and build projects, such as birdhouses, a puppet theater, and a coaster car.

5. Social studies textbooks use narratives to make history, geography, or cultures come alive. Narratives are usually found within chapters, providing a personal or human side of social studies. As a parent, you can contribute to the human interest story. Select historical fiction books from the library to complement topics being studied in social studies. Your child's teacher or librarians can help you identify some interesting historical fiction books. Look at your child's textbooks. Sometimes at the end of textbook chapters additional readings, such as historical fiction, are listed.

Chapter 5

PUTTING MOTIVATION to WORK

Reading is a skill which can be continually developed throughout life. As you read more and more about any one topic, you become a more skillful reader. Your reading rate increases, and understanding and remembering information also improves. Vocabulary expands and becomes a natural part of your reading, speaking, and writing. Unless you stop reading, these skills will continue to develop and improve. Therefore, your goal is to give your child the stimulation to become a lifelong reader.

Developing Your Child into a Lifelong Reader

Motivation, a positive attitude, and interest in reading need to be developed and nurtured if your child is to become a lifelong reader. As a parent, you can be a great motivating force. Try some of the following techniques and watch your child develop into a lifelong reader.

• Sharing Books

Read to your child no matter how old he is. Read and share magazines, comic strips, and newspapers. Talk about interesting books you have read as a child. Also, make a point of reading and discussing some contemporary books. As times change and our world becomes more complex, children's reading interests also change. You need to be sensitive to these changes and encourage the exploration of contemporary issues through reading. There are several good resources to help you select good reading materials for sharing. A good way to keep current with new children's books is to talk to the local children's librarian who can provide you with titles and book summaries as well as direct you to books most popular with children. The International Reading Association publishes a bibliography of children's books that are favorites of more than 10,000 children. To receive this book list, send a self-addressed (6½ by 9½ inch) stamped envelope to "Children's Choices," International Reading Association, 800 Barksdale Road, P.O. Box 8139, Newark, Delaware 19714. Another good resource for selecting good children's books is the *Reading Rainbow Gazette,* a newspaper for children and parents that reviews quality children's books.

• Surrounding Your Child with Books

To become excited about reading, children need to have books in their home. A book makes a good present and an even more exciting one if it is autographed by the author. The greater the number and variety of books, the more likely it is that reading will catch his interest. Funny books, puzzles, game books, fiction books, non-fiction books, magazines, tall tales, jokes, mysteries, etc. should be a part of your child's book collection. Not all of these books need be hardbound. Paperbacks are just as good and much less expensive. Children seem to enjoy paperbacks as much if not more than hardbound ones. An inexpensive way to achieve a large children's library is to purchase books at garage sales, library sales, or used-book stores.

• Enjoying the Library Together

In addition to his personal library, your child needs to have his own library card. There is no way parents can visualize the book characters in the same way as they appeared in the movie? TV movies may also encourage your child to read other books by the same author. Or they may encourage your child to find biographies or magazines about his favorite movie and TV personalities.

There are many television programs that increase your child's knowledge of the world, programs such as "Nova," "National Geographic," "Bits and Bytes," et cetera. These and other educational programs are predominantly found on the Public Broadcasting Station, PBS. These days educational programs like those found on PBS are exciting and stimulating and can make reading easier. The more knowledge your child has on a topic, the easier it is to read and learn more about it. Educational programs can also develop new interests or hobbies for your child and motivate him to read further.

PBS educational programs, such as "Sesame Street" and "Electric Company," are specifically designed for children. An exceptional PBS children's program is "Reading Rainbow," in which dance, music, and theater are used to entice children to visit their library and read its many wonderful books. Each show has a featured book narrated by a famous TV personality. The children not only hear the story but also enjoy the book's illustrations. The show includes background information on different places, events, and concepts found in the featured book. "Reading Rainbow" has attracted approximately 6.5 million viewers. There is even a newspaper published by the show's producers called the *Reading Rainbow Gazette* that contains information for both parents and children, including reading activities related to the show's featured books. Summaries of the featured books and bibliographic information are included so children can easily acquire these books from their local libraries and bookstores. Encourage your child to watch this program and other educational programs that can help him better understand and enjoy books. TV doesn't have to be a wasteland. If programs are critically selected, TV can stimulate reading and help to develop the reading habit.

- Solving Problems By Reading

Your child is naturally curious about his world. How are babies made? How do airplanes fly? What makes the sun rise? These and other questions awaken your child's interest and can be answered by reading books. But your child must be made aware that books can answer questions and solve problems so that he will naturally turn to them to seek answers. Try this activity! Sit down and discuss some topics about which your child is curious. Make a list of questions about the topics. Go to your local library and together use the subject index of the card catalog. Select and locate the appropriate books. Use the book's index or table of contents to find the answer. Skim the page to see if the answer appears on this page. If so, carefully reread to better understand the answer. This is an easy technique for children to use on their own..

- Praising Reading Efforts

If you expect your child to read, you need to take notice. Praise his efforts even if he doesn't understand everything or if he pronounces some words incorrectly. Spend some time helping him understand and teach him the correct pronunciations.

Some children need additional incentives to develop a love for reading. You may need to establish a system of rewards. Discuss with your child the reward he would like to receive for reading a certain number of books. Make the goal achievable. Let him choose his own books. As your child becomes more involved, he'll begin to read for fun rather than for a reward.

- Parents as Avid Readers

One of the most effective techniques to develop lifelong reading is your personal use of informational books. Do you use books to learn and find out answers to perplexing problems? For example, do you remember the obtain the wide selection of books that a library offers. Children will learn to love the library if you make checking out books a regular family activity. Encourage your child to select his own library books for leisure-time reading. Forcing your child to read "classics" or "must read" books is not the answer. Many times it causes children to turn away from reading in favor of other activities. Remember, your child will become a good reader if he reads frequently, so let him choose his own books. You can suggest books you found enjoyable to read at his age, but don't pressure him to read them if he's not interested.

Unfortunately, too many times, as parents, we visit the library only when called on to help with school reports. The scenario goes something like this: It is Friday, late afternoon, and the report is due on Monday. Carey and her mother have many errands to do before dinner. They barely have fifteen minutes to find some books on the report on states required for social studies. Wouldn't you know it, several other fifth-grade classrooms are studying the states. Most of the books have been checked out. Those remaining are old and too difficult to read. Carey frowns, folds her arms, and shrugs her shoulders. She doesn't seem to be motivated. Carey's mother is beginning to lose her patience. You can easily predict how the story ends. Such a negative parent-child experience can hardly be beneficial for developing a lifelong reader. If these situations occur regularly, your child will associate the library only with school work and not with relaxation and enjoyment.

Visit the library during leisure time. This is a time for you and your child to relax and enjoy together. Don't wait until an assignment has been made at school. The assignment may require your assistance, but don't let it be the only time you and your child go to the library.

• Tying Your Child's Interests to Reading

Any hobby, sport, vacation, etc. can develop the lifelong reading habit. For example, a family vacation to a different state provides an excellent opportunity to research your trip. Places to visit, the history of the area, and ways to get there are possible reading suggestions. Also, it's a perfect opportunity to develop map-reading skills!

Besides books, there are magazines on your child's hobbies, sports, and vacation spots. Children enjoy magazines. They offer a different format that provides novelty and variety. They are also short and quick to read. Many photographs and illustrations are included, making them interesting to read.

Encourage your child to join organizations that develop his interests. Many organizations offer reading material for their members, such as newsletters or magazines. Being a member of an organization provides an incentive to read organizational materials.

Your focus on your child's interest is naturally motivating to him. Learning is developed in a natural way because it is rooted in personal experiences and nourished and developed through books and magazines.

• Family Reading

The reading habit can be further developed by establishing reading as a regular daily or weekly family activity. Create comfortable surroundings for reading. Beanbag or other comfortable chairs can entice many children to read. A pleasant room, well lighted and ventilated, with books, magazines, and newspapers, will encourage reading. You may want to arrange time to talk about the interesting things each family member has been reading. Discussions will help perpetuate reading interests and develop new ones.

• Combining TV with Reading

You may be surprised to learn that TV can be a good source for developing lifelong readers. Many times a movie on TV can entice your child to read the book version. What a perfect opportunity to compare the book to the TV movie! Was the plot changed? Did your child last time you wanted new wallpaper for your kitchen but you didn't have the slightest idea of how to wallpaper? Did you look for books to help you learn? Did your child see you selecting the right book and studying it? This is important! If you use books to find answers, so will your children. Parents serve as models to their children, and it is a powerful way to develop desired behaviors.

Of all these suggestions for developing a lifelong reader, the most important is that you use books. Read frequently so your child sees the importance and enjoyment you receive from reading. Such experiences will foster the reading habit as well as improve your child's reading skills. There is nothing like practice to improve skills. And so it is with reading—practice does indeed make perfect.

Community Resources
that Contribute to Lifelong Reading

The Public Library

Your community library can be an endless source of information and services for your child and family. Most libraries have a section especially designed for children and young adults as well as librarians who are trained specifically in their literature. Usually the library has programs for children of all ages. Preschoolers can be involved in a weekly story hour during which the librarian reads good children's picture books aloud. Summer programs are usually offered to encourage the reading habit. A variety of activities are scheduled and prizes awarded to provide additional incentives to read. Check with your local library for the programs available for your child.

Libraries usually have evenings when films are shown for the whole family. Again, this is a good opportunity for stimulating your child to read the book version of a film. Also, more and more libraries are purchasing and renting films, video-tapes, and records which can further enhance your child's reading interests. Listening to the musical score of a movie may encourage your child to read the corresponding book. Computers are also being purchased by libraries, and there are a number of software programs to develop reading skills, such as vocabulary, word identification, and comprehension. This can be a good supplement for continuing your child's reading development. To find out the complete services available to your child, contact your community library.

Museums

Typically, museums sponsor educational programs that usually consist of tours, reading materials, and sometimes courses for families. Museums can initiate a child's interests or perpetuate and expand his interests. To obtain information about the resources available to your family, contact the museum in your area for a schedule of events and educational opportunities for your family.

To locate specific museums in your area, check your bookstore or library for directories that list museums and summaries of exhibits and services. Address, phone number, and contact person are usually included. The local chamber of commerce is another source for locating museums, and you may want to check your local Yellow Pages.

Other Community Resources

Besides museums, you can visit places like the botanic gardens, conservatories, wild life preserves, arboretums, et cetera. These community resources can provide your child with new knowledge about a special interest or can inspire new interests. Each of these resources also offers tours, reading materials, and educational programs. What a perfect opportunity for the whole family to enjoy learning together!

The theater is another opportunity that will inspire children to read. Children's productions, such as "The Nutcracker Suite," "The Wizard of Oz," and others, may act as catalysts for reading the actual plays. In some communities, there are opportunities for children to take part in play productions. What a valuable and enjoyable experience for children! If your child is part of a cast, he will not only read the actual play, but he'll develop a better understanding of the characters and plot. He must learn to use facial expressions and body movements to portray the character. Production elements, such as costumes, stage crew, scenery, etc., can open doors to new interests for your child.

Plays can provide your child with opportunities for learning that can't be developed through other methods. An actual experience that illustrates this point happened to a fourth-grade boy whom I'll call Jeff. He was experiencing some very real reading difficulties and making slow progress in a remedial reading program. Jeff was interested in acting and excited about the forthcoming fourth- and fifth-grade production of *Huckleberry Finn.* Of course, he wanted the lead role of Huck Finn! A leading role always has a tremendous number of lines, and this was no different, thus seeming to present problems to a disabled reader. But Jeff had his heart set on the lead, so he practiced the part by reading and rereading Huck Finn's lines. His determination and hard work got him the role! On the day of tryouts, Jeff not only knew Huck's lines, but also understood Huck.

A nice ending to this story is that Jeff not only did an excellent job in the role of Huck but also became a competent reader. Shortly after the play, he no longer needed a remedial reading program. This may not always happen, but it is another way to motivate children.

The School's Role in Developing a Lifelong Reader

Schools need to develop skilled readers, but they also must be concerned with creating a love for reading. If they don't, children will not become lifelong readers and will be robbed of a continual increase in their reading skills. But, even worse, they will not experience the beauty, love, and enjoyment reading brings to people of all ages. See if your child's teacher is incorporating the following points to increase your child's love of reading.

1. Does reading instruction match your child's abilities? Your child needs to be challenged, but not frustrated. If reading instruction is too easy, he may become bored and disinterested. When instruction is too difficult, children tend to give up and avoid reading. Either way your child loses.

2. Is your child reading interesting materials? Interesting reading is motivational. When your child finds the stories in his reading program dull, it is time for you to study these materials, keeping in mind your child's critical comments. If his criticisms are valid, discuss them with your child's teacher.

3. Does your child select stories or books for reading instruction? To motivate children to read, there should be opportunities for your child to self-select some stories and books for reading instruction. In subjects such as history and science, many times children are expected to write research reports. If they can self-select their topics, motivation is improved and a better report is achieved.

4. Is time given for free reading? A recreational reading period is motivational and creates good reading attitudes. This is especially true if children can choose their own reading materials. Many schools now employ free-reading and may call it "Sustained Silent Reading" or "SSR" (developed by McCracken).

5. Is your child encouraged to share what he has read? Sharing thoughts and feelings about books can be stimulating and inspirational. This exchange is good for encouraging children to read and becomes a contagious, enjoyable experience for all involved. Along with free-reading, many schools provide time for sharing books. Children meet in small groups to discuss their favorite characters or authors. What better way to develop reading for pleasure!

6. Is your child critically reviewing books? Another common practice in schools is to have children read, evaluate, and recommend books to others of their own age. Many times, children value the recommendation of another child above an adult's recommendation.

7. Is your child encouraged to write to authors? Writing and listening to a favorite author can be an awe-inspiring experience. Many children's authors will answer letters from youngsters, and many also accept speaking engagements. What a good activity for a local parent-teacher organization to sponsor!

8. Is your child regularly reading other children's writing? Children like to read their friends' writing. Consequently, teachers can capitalize on this by having children share their stories and reports. Being an author can motivate reading as well as writing. In some states, there are young authors' conferences. Schools hold local conferences and then choose children's stories to be included in the state conference. In these conferences, children not only write, but illustrate and bind their books so they look professional. Even in areas where young authors' conferences do not exist, teachers can help children make their stories into books. Illustrations and book binding are part of being an author. Bookmak-

ing adds a final touch and encourages children to read as well as write.

9. Since TV is part of our world and children love to watch it, is your child's school using TV to enhance and motivate learning? More and more TV producers are encouraging educators to use specific TV programs to develop children's learning. Teaching materials based on TV programs and stressing comprehension, vocabulary, and writing skills are sent to schools. The purpose is to encourage program viewing as well as to enhance class instruction. Many of these programs are based on books, so children are encouraged to read and compare the book with the program.

10. Does your child's teacher read to the children? Last, but certainly not least, reading aloud can motivate your child to read. It can expand his horizons and allow him to experience new places, people, and events. It is a key to developing lifelong reading.

The Role of Community Resources in the School

Community resources can play a supportive role in learning in our schools and help to stimulate growth in reading. Does your child's school use these resources to motivate reading and learning? Can parents play a role in combining community resources with school learning? Evaluate the first question by talking to your child, his teacher, and principal. Parent-teacher organizations can help plan, organize, and finance community resource activities that can support and stimulate school learning. Both parent and teacher can be involved in the planning. Here are a few suggestions to use community resources for increasing learning. Don't let these limit your own creative ideas.

1. Local cultural groups may provide educational services to schools. If there is a local symphony in the area, its representatives or members may provide concerts, exhibitions, or lectures. Art leagues may provide schools with art exhibitions on certain artists or art periods. Local theater groups may also perform or provide lectures and demonstrations about theater.

2. Many parents or adults in the community may be interested in sharing their hobbies or skills with school-aged children. Organizing a parent speaker directory can be a valuable aid and welcome resource for schools.

3. Local clubs may be willing to provide speakers. Garden clubs, international groups, boating organizations, etc. may be interested in providing their services to schools.

4. Local merchants and industries may offer tours or speakers to discuss their businesses.

5. Identify children's favorite authors. Contact the author or publisher to speak to your child's school. Listening and talking to authors can do wonders to stimulate children's reading and writing.

Community resources can serve as a springboard to reading. Learning about a topic, hobby, or skill may cause children to use the school or public library to seek out additional information. But, as a parent, you may need to spur your child to search for books on his topics of interest. Children need to learn that books are their most valuable source.

Suggestions for Parents

1. A good motivating activity is "Reader's Theater" in which scenery, action, and characters are imagined. Characters' parts are only read rather than memorized. No scenery or costumes are made.

2. Suggest to your child that he design book jackets for his own books.

3. The International Reading Association has pamphlets available for promoting reading to children. You can obtain them at no cost from IRA by sending a self-addressed stamped envelope to:

> International Reading Association
> 800 Barksdale Road
> P.O. Box 8139
> Newark, Delaware 19711

Try these titles from IRA:

> "Summer Reading is Important"
> "You Can Use Television to Stimulate Your Child's Reading Habits"
> "Good Books Make Reading Fun for Your Child"
> "You Can Encourage Your Child to Read"

4. Display your child's own stories and pictures of stories and books he has read.

5. Submit your child's writing to children's magazines. The following are a few magazines that publish children's work. Request a copy of the publisher's guidelines before submitting your child's writing.

> *Child Life* (ages 7-11), 1100 Waterway Boulevard, P.O. Box 567B, Indianapolis, IN 46206

> *Children's Playmate* (ages 3-8), 1100 Waterway Boulevard, P.O. Box 567B, Indianapolis, IN 46206

> *Cricket,* P.O. Box 100, LaSalle, IL 61301

> *Current Events,* 245 Long Hill Road, Middletown, CT 06457

Ebony Jr!, 820 S. Michigan Avenue, Chicago, IL 60605

Highlights for Children, 803 Church Street, Honesdale, PA 18431

Kids for Ecology (Grades K-9), P.O. Box P-7126, Philadelphia, PA 19117

Read (Grades 6-9), 245 Long Hill Road, Middletown, CT 06457

Stone Soup (ages 4-12), Box 83, Santa Cruz, CA 95063

"NOPE. TRY AGAIN."

Chapter 6

SCHOOL TESTING
WHAT DOES IT MEAN *?*

Has your child brought home tests with letter grades such as A, B, C? Can you remember receiving computerized results with scores of 5.6 and 55 percentile? Or maybe your child has brought home tests with "mastered" on them. These are all examples of test results. Although they all are quite different from one another, each can provide helpful information.

Tests come in a variety of forms, some of which are formal with computerized scores in each of the subject areas. More informal tests report their results in letter grades, percentages, or points. These tests are often teacher-made and specific to a school subject or topic and may be concerned with diagnosing strengths and weaknesses in subject area skills, such as reading or mathematics. Other tests are concerned with a child's achievement.

As you read, you're probably forming some questions about testing. Are some of the following questions yours?

- What is the purpose of testing?
- What do test scores mean?

- Is my child progressing at a normal rate?
- Is he reading on grade level like others his age?
- What are his strengths and weaknesses?
- How can I help him do better on tests?

Why Test?

Let's first consider the purposes for testing children. Tests provide several pieces of information that help teachers better educate children. Teachers use tests to assess and compare your child's achievement with other children his age. Test results are used to compare achievement in your child's school to other schools across the country. Tests can provide information to better evaluate the school's educational programs in areas like reading and mathematics. Testing is used to discover if your child has learned the content and skills in the classroom. And, lastly, testing is needed to diagnose your child's strengths and weaknesses in learning.

Types of Tests: What They Can and Can't Tell You

Your child will encounter three different types of tests during his schooling. They are: standardized tests, informal tests, and criterion-referenced tests. Each of these tests are important and serve a different purpose.

Standardized Tests

A standardized test identifies your child's reading achievement in several skill areas, such as phonics, vocabulary, and comprehension. Standardized test scores compare your child's achievement to others his age across the country. Many times, there are additional scores comparing your child's reading achievement to children his age in the local school district. A different reading test is developed for each grade level with a standard set of directions and, usually, time limitations. There are two kinds of standardized tests: group and individual.

Let's first consider the group test. In a standardized group test, children usually answer multiple choice or true-false questions on a computerized scoring grid like the one shown below.

	(T)	(F)			:: ::KEY
1	:A:	:B:	:C:	:D:	:E:
2	:A:	⊂B:	⊂C:	:D:	:E:
3	:A:	:B:	:C:	:D:	:E:
4	⊂A:	:B:	⊂C:	⊂D:	⊂E:
5	:A:	:B:	:C:	:D:	:E:
6	:A:	:B:	⊂C:	⊂D:	⊂E:
7	:A:	:B:	:C:	:D:	:E:
8	:A:	⊂B:	⊂C:	⊂D:	⊂E:
9	:A:	:B:	:C:	:D:	:E:
10	:A:	⊂B:	⊂C:	⊂D:	⊂E:
11	:A:	:B:	⊂C:	⊂D:	⊂E:

The test is computer scored, and the number of correct answers is tallied to obtain the child's "raw score." Each raw score is compared to nationwide scores of other children and is usually reported as a grade equivalency, percentile, and stanine.

Grade equivalency results are the least reliable and the least useful. This score is reported using grade and month of the school year. If your child is in the third grade and obtains a grade equivalency score of 5.6, this means your child has the same number of correct answers on the reading test as a child who is in the sixth month of fifth grade. It doesn't mean your child can read fifth grade materials. What you can accurately interpret from this score is your child is a good reader and is doing better than most children his age.

The percentile is a better score for understanding your child's reading achievement because it provides a more accurate picture. The percentile indicates the position of your child's score in relation to other children's scores within the same grade level. A percentile score of 70 means that out of 100 children, 69 have scores lower and 30 have higher scores. In this case, a percentile score of 70 represents an above-average score for that specific grade level. In percentile scoring, comparisons are only made at the same grade level. As a parent, you can readily see how your child's reading compares with children at the same grade level across the country.

Stanines are the most accurate indicator of your child's true achievement level. Unlike grade equivalency and percentiles, stanines have a margin of error built into the reported score. The stanine, like the percentile, indicates the scoring position of your child in relation to other children within the same grade level. However, this score is not as precise as the percentile — each unit in the stanine scale represents a broader range of reading achievement. A stanine score can range from 1-9 with one the lowest, nine the highest, and 4, 5, 6 considered average. If your child's score is at either extreme (a 1 or 9), he is functioning either at the lowest or highest level in comparison to others at his same grade level.

To better understand stanines, let's look at the bell curve pictured below. This curve indicates positions of all children's test scores. Most of the scores are found around the center or highest point of the curve. If you look at stanines 4, 5, and 6, you'll notice 17%, 20%, and 17% appearing directly above these stanines. These percentages indicate the number of children achieving the same test scores. If you add 17%, 20%, and 17%, your total is 54% indicating that more than half of the children are achieving within this range. Thus, if your child receives a stanine of 4, 5, or 6, you can interpret his reading achievement as average for his grade level. If he receives a stanine of 7, your child's reading achievement is considered above average for his grade level because only 12% of the children obtained these same scores. You can use this bell curve for any stanine score from any test. Keep it handy; you'll find it helpful!

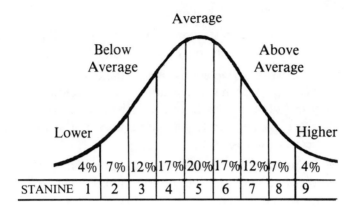

Average

Below Average	Above Average

Lower	Higher

4%	7%	12%	17%	20%	17%	12%	7%	4%
STANINE 1	2	3	4	5	6	7	8	9

The most valuable information obtained from group standardized tests is the comparison of your child's reading achievement to others within the same grade level. Your child's score is compared to other children within the country from varied ethnic, social, and economic backgrounds. This indicates your child's national standing based on national norms, which reflect the average performance of children in his grade. Your child's score may also be compared at a local level (children attending different schools within the same school district being compared). Hopefully, your child's school reports both national and local scores. You can obtain valuable information about your child's reading abilities if you are given his scores at a national and local level. For example, he may be an above average reader nationally but only average locally.

Scores from a group standardized test provide general rather than specific information. They don't pinpoint strengths and weaknesses within each skill area of reading but indicate only general strengths and weaknesses. For example, a group standardized test can indicate your child's difficulties with comprehension but will not pinpoint specifics, such as weaknesses in understanding facts or inferences.

When analyzing your child's reading scores, think about these points:

- A standardized test score captures your child's reading achievement only at one point in time.

- The score is affected by other factors besides ability, such as health, attitude, and attention. Thus, if your child is feeling sick the day he takes the achievement test, his score may not truly reflect his achievement.

- Standardized tests tend to test children's factual knowledge and some inferential abilities but do not measure children's abilities to apply knowledge. Thus, standardized tests have limitations to what they can assess in reading.

- One last caution—standardized group tests tend to report frustration reading scores. The test material is at the upper limits of your child's reading abilities.

As compared to group tests, individual standardized tests report the same scores: grade equivalency, percentiles, and stanines. But they do provide more detailed and precise information about a child's abilities. These tests tend to be diagnostic and indicate strengths and weaknesses within specific areas. Thus, individual tests usually provide a better picture of your child's capabilities than group standardized tests. The basic limitation of an individual test is the enormous amount of time it takes to administer to a single child.

Now that you can interpret results from standardized tests, you may wonder what these tests look like. Let's explore four common reading areas that are tested: phonics, vocabulary, comprehension, and rate. For each of these areas, we'll look at a commonly used group standardized reading test.

In a phonics test, the child usually compares sounds in the test word to the sounds in the several choices provided. For example, in the *Stanford Diagnostic Reading*

Test the child is required to select the word that has the same sound associated with the underlined portion of the left-hand word. In the first example, the "h" is underlined. The child must identify the word that has the same "h" sound as in "hold." The correct answer is "hair." The child has to focus on *sound* rather than *letter* — otherwise he may choose "hour." Let's look at the second example in which the "j" is underlined. The correct answer is "page." The child must be able to identify the sound at the beginning, middle, or end of the word. In this case, the "j" sound occurs in the middle of the word.

h̲old	hair	hour	mother
j̲am	ago	page	bag

In a vocabulary test, the child usually has to choose a word which has the same meaning as the test word or a word that best matches the given definition. Let's look at a specific example taken from the *Stanford Diagnostic Reading Test*. Notice the choices are highly related to each other, making it harder to choose the correct answer.

The first growth of a plant is sometimes called a
    sprout   seed   stem.

A piece of ice hanging from the roof is an
    ice cube   iceberg   icicle.

A graph is a type of
    letter   puzzle   chart.

In testing comprehension, the child usually has to read a short passage and answer multiple choice questions. Let's consider a specific example from the *Stanford Diagnostic Reading Test* that requires the child to read and answer questions. Notice the answer can be obtained by referring back to the passage. Little interpretation is required. Mainly, the child has to be able to answer factual questions. This provides a limited view of a child's comprehension capabilities.

Ann's uncle gave her a plant one day last spring. It was very small. Her uncle said, "Remember that plants need good soil, water, and sunshine. It doesn't hurt if you talk to them, either." Ann took good care of her plant. She watered it and made sure the soil was the best. She put it in the sunniest part of her room. She even told it jokes, but it never grew. Slowly, it turned brown and died. Ann decided that she must not have a green thumb.

    6.   Where did Ann Keep her plant?
- ☐ In the kitchen
- ☐ In the basement
- ☐ In her room
- ☐ In the dining room

To test reading rate, the child usually reads a passage for a short timed period and marks the word he last read. Then he answers the questions. Usually the testing company uses both the number of words and the number of correct responses to determine the child's reading rate.

A few additional points need to be made regarding standardized testing. The content of a standardized test is not specifically testing what is learned in school. It measures what is learned both inside and outside of school. Check with the teacher to learn the year that the norms or national test scores like grade equivalency, percentile, and stanine scores were established. The more recent the national norms, the greater meaning your child's test results have. Ask, "What kinds of children took the test to develop these national norms? Were they White, Black, and Chicano? Were they from upper, middle, and lower classes?" Children from your family's cultural and ethnic background and economic status should be included in the development of national norms. If not, the test may be biased and may not accurately identify your child's achievement.

Informal Tests

Throughout elementary school, your child will take many informal reading tests. The purpose of informal testing is to identify children's abilities in using classroom reading materials. Their strengths and weaknesses in word recognition, vocabulary, and comprehension are usually considered. By interpreting test results, the teacher can determine a child's progress or lack of progress and provide appropriate instruction. The beauty of informal tests is the flexibility they provide teachers. Unlike standardized tests, the teacher can modify the test instructions, provide different test examples, etc., to accurately identify a child's reading abilities. However, the teacher who administers informal tests must be knowledgeable and skilled about reading so the appropriate information for improving instruction is acquired.

A frequently used informal test is the informal reading inventory that consists of word lists and passages graded from first to eighth grade. The child reads the word lists aloud, and then the teacher can determine his strengths and weaknesses in phonics and sight words. After the word lists are concluded, the teacher administers graded passages that are usually 100 words in length and include ten questions related to the meaning of the passage. The child orally reads the passages and answers the questions until independent, instructional, and frustration reading levels are attained.

The independent level is the level at which a child can read text smoothly with few oral reading errors and with superior comprehension. In terms of scoring, for every 100 words a child reads, there should be only one, two, or three reading errors which change the meaning of the passage. The child should correctly answer nine out of ten questions. Look at the following passage containing fifty words. The markings indicate the child's oral reading errors. Which of these errors change the meaning of the passage?

Carol went shopping and saw a coat in the win-

pretty

dow. She thought that the coat was a ~~beautiful~~ one

mom
and called her ~~mother~~ over to see it. Carol's mother

saw the coat, and thought it was pretty too. Carol

was happy that her mother liked this coat. Carol

bought it.

Does the word "pretty" have a similar meaning to "beautiful?" Does "mom" mean the same as "mother?" In both cases, it appears there is no change in the passage's meaning. The child's oral reading of this passage is excellent. If he comprehends the story well, then this passage is considered his independent level.

The instructional level is one in which the child needs help from a teacher or parent in recognizing words, understanding vocabulary, or comprehending text. However, the child does not seem discouraged and can improve with instruction. In terms of scoring, the child would make about five errors for every 100 words read orally. Again, an error is counted if it changes the meaning of the passage. Additionally, the child needs to respond correctly to seven of ten comprehension questions.

At the frustration level the child needs so much help that instruction cannot be profitable. The child stumbles over many words. Oral reading is not smooth. Fidgeting and other distractible behaviors occur. The child makes ten or more meaningful errors in a 100-word passage. Only five or fewer of the ten comprehension questions are correctly answered. No child should experience such a reading experience. Too much struggling with meaning and word recognition can cause him to be "turned-off."

After teachers administer the informal reading inventory, reading levels are designated. The teacher analyzes the test results, identifying strengths and weaknesses in oral reading and comprehension. For example, she looks for repeated errors in using phonics or consistent incorrect answers to inferential questions. From these interpretations, she can devise a blueprint for reading instruction.

Talk to your child's classroom teacher and find out specifically what types of informal tests have been administered and their results. It is important that you, as a parent, know your child's three reading levels. Then you can help him select appropriate books that match his recreational (or independent) reading level. One of the best ways for your child to improve his reading skills is to immerse himself in independent reading.

It is also important for you to know your child's strengths and weaknesses so that you can help at home. Direct your instruction to your child's weaknesses. Use the appropriate activities suggested in other chapters of this book to further your child's reading development.

Other oral or written informal tests may be teacher-made and may cover such areas as phonics, sight words, vocabulary, and comprehension. Try to obtain the results of these tests, too, so you can be an educational partner in teaching your child to read.

Criterion-Referenced Tests

More and more school children are taking reading tests that measure whether or not a specific skill objective has been learned. Let's look at a typical objective in which your child may be tested.

> Given a short passage, the student will identify in writing the main idea of the passage.

To measure if a child has accomplished this objective, a criterion-referenced test is developed by a teacher, school district, or publisher. To master the objective, the child has to achieve a certain percentage of correct test responses. Once the objective is mastered, the student progresses to the next objective. There are a large number of objectives and corresponding tests at each of the elementary grade levels.

Not all schools use a criterion-referenced system of testing since this type of testing is usually associated with a specific theory of how children learn to read. The criterion-referenced system is based on the concept that reading can be broken down into separate skills that can be taught and tested. Once a child has succeeded in passing each tested skill, he should be a proficient reader. As we discussed in Chapter One, reading is not a list of distinctly separated skills. Many of these skills are so closely related, educators can't identify where one skill begins and another ends. Reading is complex. It requires the simultaneous use of word recognition, vocabulary, and comprehension skills. Even the beginning reader uses all of these reading skills simultaneously.

However, many educators, knowing that reading is too complex to break down into bits and pieces, rely on a test score in reporting to parents because it is specific and easily understood. Many educators note that even though reading can't be broken down into many small parts, criterion-referenced test results provide parents with some understanding of how their child is progressing in school. Be cautious! Even though your child passes each mastery test, it doesn't necessarily mean he is a good reader. You must look at other tests, such as standardized and informal results, to determine if your child is becoming a proficient reader.

However, there is a positive characteristic of criterion-referenced tests. It is possible that *all* children taking the test can master the objectives, while in standardized reading tests, some children must be labeled as failures and others as superior readers.

Improving Your Child's Test-Taking Abilities

One of the best ways to help your child do better on tests is to make sure he has a nutritious breakfast and lunch. Your child can then concentrate on thinking and completing the test without the distraction of hunger. Also, a good night's sleep is necessary if your child is to be alert during testing. Recommend to your child that he try the following suggestions when he is scheduled to take the next test:

1. Relax before and during the time you are taking the test. Test anxiety does not accomplish a thing, but makes you uncomfortable and, at times, immobilizes thinking.

2. Carefully read the directions or listen attentively to the directions given. Ask questions if you are unsure what to do.

3. If the test is multiple choice or true-false, do those questions first that can be answered quickly and accurately. Then go back and do those that require some thinking.

4. If the test is multiple choice or true-false, stick to your first choice. Second guessing many times causes you to select the incorrect answer.

5. Make sure you concentrate on the test. Do not let other thoughts interrupt your thinking. Concentrating and attending to the test allows you to make clear and logical choices.

6. If you are taking an essay or short answer test, brainstorm first. Write down brief notes about possible answers or points to be made. Then go back and organize your thoughts. Delete and add any new ideas. Now you're ready to write your response. This three-step process does take a little extra time, but your answers will be far superior because your writing will be more concise, focused, and organized.

7. Before a teacher-made test is given, write out possible questions that may appear on the test. Use these questions to study for the test. Try to answer a few questions in written form. Check the answers with the text and class notes.

These points should help your child improve his test scores. Be positive and encourage your child to do well, not only on tests but on all his school work. Consistency in using good study habits and in completing regular classroom assignments is one of the best approaches for ensuring good test performance. Regular study provides your child with the opportunity to think about and reflect on concepts he's learned in class.

Suggestions for Parents

Before a test, sit down with your child and develop some questions over the area to be tested. Quiz your child. Provide feedback and help when needed.

The author wishes to extend appreciation to the publisher for the excerpts in this chapter reproduced by permission from the Stanford Diagnostic Reading Test: 2nd Edition. Copyright ©1976 by Harcourt Brace Jovanovich, Inc. All rights reserved.

Chapter 7

FROM POOR TO GOOD READER—
HERE'S HOW!

There are different ways by which you may find out that your child is experiencing difficulties in reading. Your child may be negative about going to school and look for excuses for staying home. The symptoms may be stomach aches at reading class time. He may come home from school every day disgruntled, unhappy, and out of sorts. Or, even more obvious, his grades have fallen and test scores are lower. Any of these situations can be upsetting for both you and your child. What can be done? The first step is to schedule a parent-teacher conference and discuss the observed behaviors with your child's teacher. Ask if poor reading skills are the problem, then ask her to pinpoint the troublesome areas—word identification, comprehension, oral reading, vocabulary and/or study skills. You still need additional information, so you may want to ask your child's teacher the following questions:

1. When did my child's reading problem occur?
2. How severe is this reading problem?
3. Do tests indicate my child has weaknesses in reading?

4. Can you show me examples of his work that will provide me with a better understanding of my child's weaknesses?

5. What are you doing to help my child overcome reading difficulties?

6. How can we help my child become a proficient reader?

7. Are there other problem areas?

8. Is additional diagnosis needed?

Depending on your child's age and self-concept, you may suggest to the teacher that your child also needs to be informed. He needs to understand his reading difficulties and other problem areas and how you plan to help him. Only with your child's help and cooperation can his reading problems be overcome. He will master reading when he recognizes the skills he has to develop and how these skills fit together for proficient reading. Understanding what reading is all about may bring about the "Ah-ha!" principle in learning—"Now I know what it is that I have to learn."

What is it that you, your child, and the teacher can do to overcome these reading weaknesses? An important part of the parent-teacher-child conference is designing a plan for your child's reading improvement. But before a plan is made, further diagnosis may be necessary.

Diagnosing the Disabled Reader

If your child's teacher can't pinpoint specific reading levels nor identify definite strengths and weaknesses, then further diagnosis is required. This testing may need to be administered by a reading specialist with specific training in diagnosis and remediation. The diagnosis should include both informal and individualized standardized tests. An example of a good diagnostic battery would include an informal reading inventory to establish reading levels and some strengths and weaknesses in reading.

(This is the same inventory discussed in Chapter Six.) An individualized standardized test should also be given, such as *Woodcock Reading Mastery Tests, Durrell Analysis of Reading Difficulty, Test of Reading Comprehension,* and the *Gillmore Oral Reading Test.*

If your child is in fifth grade or above, then he also needs testing in study skills. Testing in this area is best assessed informally. The reading specialist should develop an informal test, using the child's textbooks to identify his strengths and weaknesses. His ability to use the table of contents, glossary, and index should be tested as well as his ability to learn from textbooks. A thorough diagnosis should provide you and the teacher with the necessary information to begin a successful remedial reading program for your child.

The Remedial Program

When designing a remedial program, your child's three reading levels (discussed in earlier chapters) need to be pinpointed. The independent level is easy and gives your child a chance to practice reading on his own. The instructional level is challenging, but your child can learn with guided instruction. The frustration level is too difficult, so your child learns little and becomes discouraged.

The remedial program plan should answer the following questions:

1. Does the child need reading services outside the classroom with instruction by a reading specialist?

2. Or is his reading difficulty not severe enough to require outside services and can easily be corrected by the classroom teacher?

3. How long will the child need special help by either the reading specialist or the classroom teacher?

4. If special services are needed, how many times per week and for what length of time should additional help be given?

5. Is private tutoring necessary?

6. As a parent, how can I help?

If your child's reading problem is severe, then you should expect him to receive special services from the school's reading specialist. Reading two or more years below grade level is considered a severe problem. These cases require an expert's knowledge and time in order that reading improvement can be achieved with minimum time and effort. The child who is reading two or more years below grade level also needs instruction from his classroom teacher. The more instruction, the faster the progress. It is recommended that classroom and special instruction be coordinated to maximize learning and result in a shorter remedial reading program. If special instruction is necessary, then he should receive these services during the school day at least twice a week for 45 minutes. This is the minimal amount of time needed to make substantial gains in reading achievement.

If your child needs additional services from a private tutor, you need to consider coordination of instruction, time given for tutoring, and the tutor's qualifications. The private tutor must be willing to work with your child's school to coordinate reading instruction. Lack of coordination between tutor and school can lead to confusion for your child about learning to read. Your child should see this tutor twice a week for at least an hour. Once a week is not enough even if your child receives special help at school. The child needs the individual help from a private tutor for a regular and extended amount of time. Too much time elapses when your child sees his tutor only once a week, and the benefits of private tutoring diminish. When hiring a private tutor, consider the following points:

1. Does the tutor have the proper qualifications? It

is best if the tutor is a reading specialist with experience in teaching reading at your child's grade level.

2. Does the tutor have sufficient time to plan appropriate instructional lessons for your child? The tutor may hold a full-time position in a school district or other related field. You must be sure that your child will be given the planning time he needs to improve his reading skills.

3. Will the tutor talk frequently with your child's teacher? To maximize learning, regular communication is a must.

4. Does the tutor have the necessary materials to help your child become more proficient? It is not always necessary to have an abundance of new commercial materials. Library books and paperbacks can meet your child's needs. But if your child's tutor will be using commercial textbooks and workbooks, these materials should be current and appealing to today's generation. These materials must capture your child's interest; otherwise motivation and learning is negatively affected. Of course, the materials must develop learning, not just be fun.

Tutors and tutoring services can be found through newspaper advertisements, schools, the Yellow Pages, and your friends. Use the above questions to find the appropriate tutor. When interviewing tutors, make sure your child is given some input in the selection. If your child likes the tutor, it can make a difference. He'll put forth effort during the tutoring sessions.

In most cases, you, as a parent, should help your child in his efforts to improve his reading. However, I do not recommend parental assistance when the parent may not have the patience to work with a child, or the child adamantly refuses parental help. If you will be doing some supportive work at home, you need to spend some time with him discussing his feelings about being a poor reader. You want to know if and how it has affected his relationship with his friends, his feelings about himself, and his feelings toward reading and school. Be a good listener and show empathy, but not sympathy! Your child needs to be assured that even if he does not make great improvements in reading, you will still love and respect him. This kind of discussion can develop a deeper bond between you and your child. It can also provide a good beginning for remediation. Your child may need to discuss these problems again at various points during remediation. Keep the communication lines open.

To initiate a home remedial reading program, make sure you know and understand your child's strengths and weaknesses in the various reading areas. You also need to know your child's instructional level, so you can use appropriate reading materials. Ask the teacher for suggestions on materials. In most cases, your best materials are library books, paperbacks, children's magazines, and pencil and paper. (The activities suggested in the previous chapters will be helpful.) The following additional activities should help your child overcome specific problem areas. These activities are divided into four areas: comprehension, fluency, word identification, and vocabulary.

Activities to Overcome Comprehension Problems

The comprehension activities suggested in Chapter Four should develop good comprehension skills in your child. If your child has difficulty remembering major details and putting them into correct sequence, try these activities:

1. The Herringbone technique, developed by H.L. Herber, is a way to organize important pieces of information found in text. It consists of a herringbone with a series of questions. As your child reads a short two-to-four page selection, he should answer the following questions and place his answers in the appropriate spaces on the Herringbone.

1. Who is (are) the main character(s)?
2. What is (are) the character(s) doing?
3. When is the story taking place?
4. Where is the story taking place?
5. How did the problem or situation occur?
6. Why did the problem or situation occur?

From reading and responding to these questions, try to help your child formulate the main idea of the story. Look at the relationships of the five answers to develop the main idea.

The Herringbone Technique

2. The Guided Reading Procedure, developed by A.V. Manzo, can help your child develop good sequencing skills. It can also serve as as study guide for a test. Use your child's textbook and ask him to read a section of a chapter to be covered in school. For example, in a social studies text you may tell your child to read for the purpose of remembering the specific events that occurred after the bombing of Pearl Harbor. Your child reads the section silently. After silent reading is completed, ask your child to retell the events that took place after the bombing. Write the events down in phrases in the order he retells them. After the retelling is completed, your child should return to the text to check his retelling for its accuracy and completeness. Your child can add, delete, reorder, and substitute events you wrote on the paper.

Your child uses these corrected notes to study for a test. Practicing this activity often should improve your child's comprehension and grades in school.

3. As your child reads a section in his textbook, have an 8½" by 11" piece of clear plastic available. When your child comes to a part with a step-by-step process or a list of sequential events, he should place the plastic sheet over this section and with a water-based marker, write down the topic and page number. Next to each sequential step or event, place the appropriate number. Later your child can return to the text, place the plastic over the page, and reread the numbered steps or events. Now he can easily review for a test.

4. Point out to your child how authors in subject area textbooks use specific words to identify steps in a problem or events in a story. Some examples are: "in the beginning," "first," "lastly," "finally."

5. After your child has read a story, ask him to act out the events of the story. Remind him to sequence the events in the proper order.

6. Semantic Webbing, developed by G. Freeman and E.G. Reynolds, can help your child organize information from a story or textbook. To begin this activity, choose a question for your child to remember while reading the text. This question becomes the core of the web, as shown in the example below. As your child reads, he can refer to this question and jot down answers. Or he can place a light pencil mark in the margin where an answer is found.

When your child finishes reading, he writes each answer within a different circle. He shows the relationship of the question to the answer by drawing a line between them. An example is shown below.

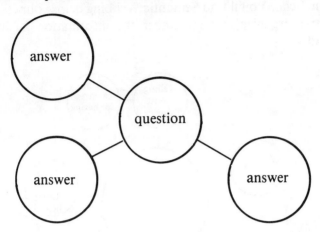

Each of your child's answers needs to have supporting evidence. Facts, inferences, and generalizations can support the answer. The supporting evidence is placed in a circle and is linked to the answer. Now the Semantic Web looks like the example below.

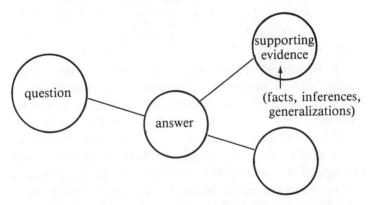

Encourage your child to make the web without referring back to the story. If this is not possible, then let him reread his notes or the story to help him develop the web.

Look at the example of a Semantic Web from the story *Ira Sleeps Over* by Bernard Waber. Notice the question has several acceptable answers. For Semantic

Webbing, it is best to ask questions that have several answers because it makes the activity more interesting and beneficial. You'll find Semantic Webbing helps your child better organize and remember the information he has read.

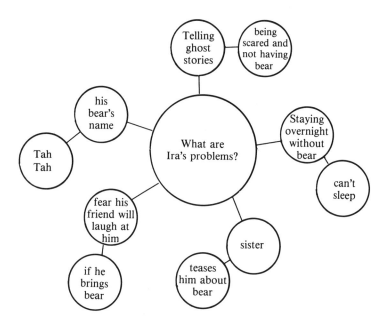

7. Paragraph frames, developed by G.L. Fowler, can help children understand summaries and ultimately be able to write their own summaries. Your role is to write a summary for a chapter in a book or an article in a magazine. Once the summary is written, delete the important details from the summary. Your child fills in the details after reading the text. Hopefully, he will not have to return to the text to fill in the blanks. However, many disabled readers, at first, will need to refer back to the text. Eventually your child should learn to fill in the blanks without looking back. An example of a paragraph frame written by S. Ridker and based on a chapter from *The Lion, The Witch, and the Wardrobe* by C.S. Lewis appears below. In this paragraph, a blank may require one or more words.

The Lion, The Witch, and The Wardrobe

In the Witch's House

Meanwhile, we find out what is happening to
_____. He is on his way to _____ and
thinking about _____. Edmund wanted ____
_____ and to be a _____and to get even with
_____ for _____. He tried to tell himself
the white witch was _____ but deep down he
knew she was really _____. As Edmund came
close to the house, he saw a dwarf and animals that
_____ by the _____. Edmund was feel-
ing _____ but he kept telling himself
_____. When the queen saw Edmund, she was
angry because _____. Edmund told her that
_____ and about _____. The queen told
the dwarf to _____ and use _____.

After your child has read the book, explain that this is a summary of Chapter Nine of *The Lion, The Witch, and The Wardrobe*. Within the summary, there are blanks that require facts from the chapter. First, read the entire summary without filling in any of the blanks. This helps your child develop an overall understanding of the summary. Now your child can start filling in the blanks. One or more words may be needed for each blank. Your child's goal is to fill in the correct facts so it makes sense when read. Help your child complete the first few blanks. Once he becomes familiar with the routine let him fill these in on his own and read it to you for your comments. For a change of pace, let him try to design his own frame for you to complete. This will provide him with the opportunity to develop his own summaries.

8. The Directed Reading-Thinking Activity (DR-TA) suggested in Chapter Four is especially helpful for developing comprehension.

9. Sequencing cartoon strips also suggested in Chapter Four is beneficial for developing good comprehension skills.

Activities to Overcome Fluency Problems

Does your child have difficulties reading smoothly?

161

Does he tend to read word-by-word or in a halting manner? Does he tend to repeat words and phrases frequently while reading orally? If these symptoms describe your child's typical reading behaviors, then fluency instruction is recommended. Try some of the following fluency activities with your child.

1. Children who can't read smoothly benefit from listening to a good "model" or reading with a good "model." The following strategy developed by C. Chomsky can help your child become a fluent reader. Provide your child with a tape recorded reading of a book he is interested in learning to read. First, tell him to listen and follow along in the book. Second, tell him to start at the beginning of the book and read along with the tape. He can stop the tape at any time to repeat sections or to take a rest before continuing. The first two steps should be repeated each day until he can read the book smoothly without tape support. At this time ask your child to discuss the story, draw a picture to explain an event or character, or do any other comprehension activity. Don't forget this last step! Your child must always remember that reading is for both understanding and enjoyment.

Learning how to read a book smoothly may take your child two or three weeks. Longer books may take more time. Each new taped book will take less time for him to read fluently.

You can acquire taped books at bookstores or libraries. You may also want to make your own tapes to go along with your child's favorite stories. Your child will probably enjoy listening and reading along with your voice.

When making a tape, read smoothly, but not too fast. Fast reading tends to be frustrating for the follow-along reader. Use a bell or other sound to signal that a new page is to be read. Your child may need to be told the page number so he can easily keep his place. Remember to pause long enough between pages so your child can easily turn the page and resume reading.

Your child's interest and cooperation in this activity are keyed to his personal selection of the book or passage to be taped. Let him select the book even if it seems too difficult. The support of the tape overcomes the difficulty of the text.

If your child chooses books containing many chapters, tape one chapter at a time. When your child can read the chapter fluently, ask him some questions to develop understanding.

To show your child his oral reading progress, tape record his first reading. After a few days, tape his reading of the same text. Let him compare and discuss the changes in his oral reading. Your child will enjoy listening to his improved reading.

2. "Repeated Readings," developed by S.J. Samuels, is a short and quick activity for developing fluent reading. Select an easy and interesting 50-200 word passage. Ask your child to read the passage as smoothly as possible. Time his oral reading and count the errors he makes. Count only those errors that change the meaning of the passage. Reading "pretty" for "beautiful" does not greatly alter the meaning of the passage and should not be counted as an error. At the end of the reading, record the number of words per minute and the number of errors. Conclude the reading by asking your child at least one comprehension question.

Before attempting another repeated reading, your child may need some help with identifying unknown words or understanding the passage. Spend some time providing this kind of help. Continue to reread the same passage until he can read 85 words per minute and makes very few errors. Once he has accomplished this task, your child can begin a new passage.

Keep a chart of the number of rereadings. You can make a bar graph to represent the number of words per minute achieved in each attempt. The graphs help your child easily see progress. To stress the importance of comprehension, be sure you ask one comprehension question after each attempt.

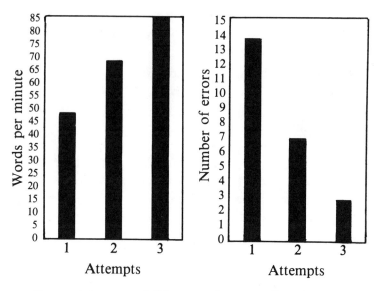

For variety, your child may enjoy rereading the passage into a tape recorder. He can listen to his own reading, checking for smooth reading and word identification errors. Your child's analysis of his oral reading abilities can be beneficial to growth in learning.

3. Choral reading develops smooth oral reading skills. Select a passage with rhythm. Poetry and music are good beginning selections. You and your child will read the poem or lyrics simultaneously as if you were in a chorus. In this particular case, you are in a speaking chorus rather than a singing chorus. Choral reading can be fun. Keep practicing until you can perform it well for the rest of your family. Family performances can be enjoyable and a reason for continual practice. You may want to try first some poems from Shel Silverstein's books *Where the Sidewalk Ends* and *The Light in the Attic.*

4. If your child is experiencing extreme difficulties with fluency, try "echo reading." Select an interesting story written at the child's instructional or high independent level. Read a short section aloud to your child. Tell your child to repeat the same section orally. Continue reading the entire book in this same manner. First the

parent reads, then the child echoes. Remember to read only a small section aloud – for example, a paragraph. You do not want to frustrate your child by reading too much. Continue this strategy until your child begins to read smoothly. Fluency is usually developed slowly just as any other reading skill. Instill confidence in your child so he believes he will succeed. Remediation takes time and patience.

Activities to Overcome Word Identification Problems

Often poor readers need help with word identification. They can't immediately identify common words. They lack skill in using context to develop meaning of unknown words. Looking up words and choosing the right definition is often difficult. Try some of the following word identification activities. You'll find your child will become a better reader. (You may also find it helpful to review the word identification activities found in Chapters Three and Four.)

• Sight Words

Many times disabled readers have a poor sight word vocabulary. They can't instantly recognize a word that appears frequently in books. Children often miss sight words such as "house," "game," "look," et cetera. (See the list of high frequency words on page 252.) Besides learning common words, children eventually have to know all words at sight. Spending time recognizing words slows down reading and hinders comprehension. Does your child consistently miss common words? Are there too many words he spends time trying to identify? If so, many of the following sight word activities will help.

1. Your child should read very easy books containing an overabundance of high frequency words. Then repeated exposure to sight words within

context should help your child increase his speed in word identification.

2. Write on index cards those words your child continually misses. Add a set of cards with words your child knows and use both sets of cards to build sentences to read aloud.

3. Make a racetrack game as suggested in Chapter Three, but this time place unknown word cards on each space of the racetrack. Use markers and dice to move along the board. When your child lands on a space, he identifies the word. If he can't, he loses a turn. If he is successful, he can proceed along the gameboard to the finish line. Children enjoy game situations for learning. Games can be a good learning tool and a break from typical class instruction.

4. Use the game concept from "Go Fish!" to improve your child's recognition of sight words. On each pair of index cards, place a word your child can't often identify. Deal seven cards to your child and to yourself. Scatter the rest of the cards upside down between you and your child. The object of the game is to be the first player to get rid of all cards by eliminating matched pairs. To begin play, one player checks his cards to see if he has any pairs. If so, he puts those down and says the word. If he is unable to say the word, he has to "go fish"—that is, he has to select a card from those scattered in front of him. If he does not have a pair in his hand, he must automatically go fish. The game continues until one player has no more cards.

• Phonics

Phonics is another area that presents difficulties to disabled readers. But before you can help your child, gather information about his strengths and weaknesses. If your child's teacher is unable to supply such information, design your own informal test. Test only those phonic elements that are regular. These are: single consonants ("b," "c," "m," etc.), consonant clusters ("ch," "th," "sh," etc.), words that have a consonant-short-vowel-consonant form ("cat," "sit," "mop," etc.), words that have a consonant-long-vowel-consonant-silent "e" form ("date," "cake," "kite," etc.), and r-controlled vowels ("bar," "fur," "bird," etc.). See page 250 for a list of some of these words.

To test your child's knowledge of consonants and consonant clusters, place a single consonant or cluster on an index card. Ask your child to tell you two words beginning with this consonant and two words ending with the same consonant. If your child can't frequently and easily identify words for each consonant and consonant cluster, then he probably needs some instruction in consonants and/or consonant clusters.

To test the short vowel (căt) and the long vowel patterns (dātę), and r-controlled vowels (bar), use the Word Sort technique discussed in Chapter Three.

One cautionary note, some children seem to know phonics but don't apply them while reading. These children tend to skip unknown words, or ask someone to tell them the word. To learn if this is your child's problem, ask him to read a rather difficult passage and see if he uses phonics to identify unknown words. If you find your child doesn't apply phonics, then show him how to apply this knowledge when meeting unknown words in text.

If your child needs further phonics instruction, the activities in Chapter Three can improve his phonics skills. You may also want to try these additional activities:

1. Keep Word Sort cards (described in Chapter Three) available when your child is reading text. These cards can be invaluable in focusing your child's attention on the phonic element he is unable to recognize while reading. Provide your child with a reading selection. As your child

reads and comes to an unknown word in which phonics can be applied, use the Word Sort cards to contrast the similar vowel pattern of the known word to the unknown. Suggest that he first look at the Word Sort card and say that word. Now he should attempt the pronunciation of the word in text. The Word Sort cards with the following vowel patterns should be available to your child while reading text: "cat," "tip," "but," "rod," "ten," "cake," "bike," "ride," "cute." Keep these handy for your child's immediate use. The important point about phonics is to make sure your child has many opportunities to apply phonics knowledge. When your child reads text and comes to an unknown word, give him time to apply his phonic learnings before you tell him the word.

2. Many disabled readers have difficulties with vowels, and rightfully so, because these letters represent so many sounds in our English language. Look at the vowel "a" and see how many different sounds it represents in the following words: "about," "are," "cake," "cat," "each," "taught." Your child may benefit from learning vowel sounds when used in spelling patterns or word families. Use the following list of word families to substitute different beginning consonant sounds and consonant clusters. You may want to begin this activity by providing two examples of the word family such as "rage" and "cage." Tell your child to remove the "r" and the "c" from "age" and replace it with a different consonant to make a new word. Write those words down and discuss their likenesses and differences. You and your child can write sentences together using these words. Continue this activity with other word families. Here are a few word families to get you and your child started. (More word families are listed on page 249.)

<u>c</u>ab	<u>c</u>age	<u>s</u>et	<u>l</u>ike	<u>s</u>ob
<u>m</u>ad	<u>m</u>ade	<u>b</u>eg	<u>l</u>ick	<u>c</u>lock
<u>r</u>ag	<u>s</u>ack	<u>s</u>eat	<u>r</u>ide	<u>c</u>og
<u>r</u>an	<u>l</u>amp	<u>b</u>end	<u>b</u>ill	<u>r</u>od
<u>d</u>ay	<u>w</u>alk	<u>t</u>ell	<u>k</u>ite	<u>c</u>oil
<u>f</u>at	<u>c</u>ave	<u>m</u>ess	<u>d</u>ive	<u>c</u>ord
<u>s</u>ap	<u>t</u>ake	<u>m</u>eal	<u>f</u>ix	<u>b</u>ox
<u>t</u>ax	<u>f</u>arm	<u>b</u>ad	<u>m</u>iss	<u>m</u>ore

3. The next activity is based on a tried and true method developed by reading expert Robert Karlin. If your child is experiencing difficulties in learning a specific phonic element, such as "ch," this activity should help. There are four easy steps.

Step 1: Write a sentence containing a new word with the sound your child has difficulty recognizing. Underline the new word and write several familiar words sharing this same sound. Let's look at an example of this step and use it to develop steps two and three.

John and Bob were good <u>chums.</u>
chip
chime
chat

Step 2: Tell your child to pronounce the words in the column. Ask him how these words are like the underlined word in the sentence. Help him to develop the "ch" sound.

Step 3: Select word families, such as __ap, __ug, from page 249. Tell your child to blend the "ch" sound with these word endings. Here is an example.

ch + ap = chap   ch + ug = chug
ch + in = chin   ch + eat = cheat

Step 4: Ask your child to read the first sentence. Make sure he not only pronounces "chums" correctly but he also understands the meaning.

4. Many times disabled readers have difficulties with blending sounds within words. To provide your child with practice in this skill, try the following activity. List a number of two or more syllable words on a piece of paper. Look these words up in a dictionary. Write down the pronunciation of the word exactly as it appears in the dictionary. Let's look at some examples.

centerboard	sent - ər - bōrd
habitation	hab - ə - tā - shən
sentimental	sent - ə - ment - əl
value	val - yü

Tell your child to look at the word and its special pronunciation. Try to blend the syllables together to form the correct pronunciation of the word. Your child will need to use the dictionary to refer to the symbols used in the special pronunciation of the word.

• Context

To become a proficient reader, your child has to be able to use context skills. In fact, context skills are the most frequently used skills by good readers for word identification. Children, for the most part, automatically use context to recognize and understand a word. But we need to teach children to use context efficiently and accurately and not abuse it with wild guessing. Try these activities to improve your child's use of context.

1. To focus on context and eliminate guessing, tell your child to read "blank" for an unknown word and continue reading to the end of the sentence. Then ask him to look at the beginning and final

letters and associate the appropriate sounds for each. Return to the beginning of the sentence and read it, filling in the appropriate word. This context activity combines both phonics and context. The unknown word has to make sense, but also has to conform to the sounds and letters found in the unknown word. Encourage your child to use this strategy while reading on his own.

2. Copy the beginning of a selection from your child's favorite magazine and occasionally delete a word and replace it with a blank. Keep the blanks consistent in size so you do not provide your child with inappropriate clues. Tell your child the topic and tell him to read your copied portion with the blanks. Your child should not try to fill in the blanks until he has read the material once. He may skip some blanks and return to them later. It is very difficult to fill in the blanks in sequential order. Tell your child there are many words that make sense in each blank. He is to select words that develop the author's meaning. After he has finished this activity, compare his word choices with those of the author. A good discussion should take place. Remember, selecting the author's exact word is not the goal. The child should select words that make sense in the paragraphs.

3. Present your child with a sentence or sentences and underline the word he probably will not understand. Ask your child to read the entire sentence(s) to develop an understanding of the unknown word. Tell your child to draw a picture of what the word or sentence(s) means. An example of one sentence is provided below.

On the African <u>safari</u>, the hunter saw many elephants, tigers, and lions.

Your child's picture should indicate his understanding of the word, but it is also helpful if he explains his picture so you can better check word meaning.

4. Riddles can help children learn to use context clues effectively. Develop a riddle like the one below and ask your child to supply the correct word.

> I am very scaly.
> I live in water.
> I have fins.
> Who am I? _____

• Structural Analysis

To help your child become more skillful at identifying unknown words, he needs to know the meanings of some frequently used prefixes and suffixes such as those found in the following words: "**re**turn," "**sub**marine," "**un**tie," "**im**possible," "play**er**," and "cauti**ous**." These prefixes and suffixes are often found in children's textbooks and, if known, they can help children better understand text. The goal is for your child to know the meaning of prefixes and suffixes and apply it to the unknown word. But children must first know the root word's meaning if prefixes and suffixes are to be helpful. For example, let's consider the word "incomplete." If he understands the meaning for the root word "complete," and he knows that the prefix "in" means "not," then he can apply the meaning of "in" to the meaning of complete.

There are many prefixes and suffixes in the English language so it would be impossible for your child to learn all of them. Therefore, I recommend that you teach your child those prefixes and suffixes frequently used in the English language, but I do not recommend that children memorize prefix and suffix meanings. They need to learn these meanings when used in words and used in sentences.

Prefix	Example	Meaning
dis	disconnect	apart, not
ex	export	out
im	impossible	not
pre	prearrange	before
re	return	back
post	postdate	behind
super	superbomb	over and above
trans	transport	across
sub	submarine	under
un	unexcited	not

Suffix	Example	Meaning
er, or, ist	player actor activist	performer of
tion, sion	prevention tension	act of
ity, ty	hilarity misty	conditions of
ance, ence	appearance silence	state of
ble, able, ible	scramble agreeable horrible	capable of being
ment	agreement	act of, condition
ful	playful	full of
ious, ous	cautious famous	full of, posses- sing the qualities of
ly, y	merrily happily	in the manner of, like in appearance
less	worthless	without
ish	foolish	being, char- acteristic of

Use the following suggested activities to develop your child's skill in using prefixes and suffixes.

1. Place a prefix, root word, and suffix on separate cards, using the prefixes and suffixes suggested above. You and your child can make words by placing prefix, root word, and suffix cards together. Let your child experiment with placing these word parts together. He need not always use both prefixes and suffixes, just one or the other. But there must always be a root contained in his word. After he has matched a prefix or a suffix with a root word, ask him to explain the new meaning of the word. Keep adding root words as your child becomes more adept in this skill.

2. Write two sentences for your child, one with a word containing a prefix or suffix and another without the prefix and suffix. Ask your child how the prefix or suffix changes the meaning of the sentence. An example is provided.

   John *tied* his brother's shoe.

   John *untied* his brother's shoe.

3. Select a short and interesting article from the newspaper. Copy the article, but delete some prefixes and suffixes from words within the article. Place a short blank for each deletion. Ask your child to read the entire article first. Then he should reread the article and fill in the appropriate prefixes and suffixes. To check his work, he can refer to the original newspaper article.

• Dictionary

A dictionary is an important tool for your child to learn to use well. It can provide not only the meaning of a word but also its pronunciation. To use a dictionary to its

174

fullest, children need to receive instruction. First, your child needs to understand the purpose of a dictionary. Second, he needs to understand the format of the dictionary, such as alphabetical order and guide words. Third, he must learn to use the pronunciation key so he can sound out the new word. Lastly, your child needs to understand and apply the appropriate dictionary definition. The following suggested activities should help your child develop dictionary expertise.

1. Children like to decipher codes. Write a message to your child using the pronunciation of the word rather than its correct spelling. He will need to refer to the pronunciation key found in the beginning of the dictionary to read the message orally. Start with an easy message with a few short words and progress in difficulty. Here are some examples.

    hap - ē bərth - dā   (happy birthday)
    wē sȯ ā mü - vē.   (We saw a movie.)

    Make your messages more interesting by designing a treasure hunt written in code. To travel on the treasure hunt, your child has to break the code. If he is successful, he should get to his destination and find a "treasure." You can make the hunt simple or complicated, just as long as it doesn't frustrate your child.

    In using the pronunciation key, you may need to show your child how to use key words associated with the dictionary symbols, such as "a" has the sound heard in the words "day" or "fate." By using key words, children can easily identify the proper pronunciation of the unknown word.

2. To develop proficiency in finding dictionary words, play a game called "Beat Your Time." Provide a list of words and instruct your child to look up each word and identify the correct page on which it is found. Each list should contain the

175

same number of words so you can accurately compare his improvement. Begin the game by explaining that the object of the game is to find the correct page number of each word as quickly as possible. After each list is completed, you can both chart his time. A second list is given and the goal is to look up these words faster than the preceding list. Again, his time is recorded.

If you find your child doesn't know how to use the guide words found at the top of each page, teach him this skill. After instruction, try another word list. He should notice how using guide words improves his time.

While playing "Beat Your Time," you may notice your child doesn't open the dictionary to the proper place. For example, he may open the dictionary at the beginning when he is looking up the word "zebra." This is your opportunity to provide some teaching. Again, repeat with an additional word list, and your child should notice his improvement.

3. Selecting the appropriate meaning of an unknown word is a tough skill for children to learn. To help your child develop this skill, choose some words in a story that are unknown to your child. Ask him to first read the selection in its entirety. Then ask him to use a dictionary to look up some words you preselected. His task is to choose the correct dictionary meaning and explain it in his own words. In all probability, he is going to need guidance. Help him by explaining how you choose the correct meaning when more than one definition is given for a single word. You may need to do this with several words and then supply help only when necessary. Let him try to explain his logic when selecting the appropriate dictionary definition.

4. Another game for teaching guide words can be made with poster board and a deck of word

cards. Make a gameboard as pictured below.
The object of the game is to be the first player to
progress from start to finish by telling if the
selected word would be found on that page in
the dictionary. To begin the game, the first
player rolls one die and moves his piece the
number of spaces on the die. He then selects a
card from the top of the deck and answers "yes"
or "no" to whether the word would be found on
that page. If he answers correctly, then he can
continue when it is his next turn. If he misses,
then he loses one turn. Two or more players are
needed.

Word Cards

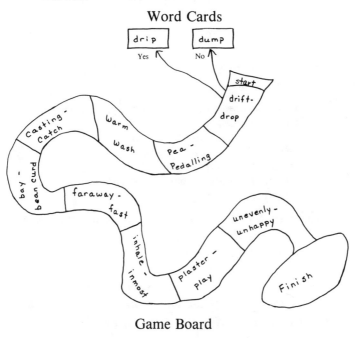

Game Board

5. Using riddles to teach dictionary skills can also
   be a lot of fun. Try these and then make up your
   own.

   Does a <u>praying</u> <u>mantis</u> pray?
   Can your aunt wear a <u>lady's</u> <u>slipper</u>?

Does a lamprey shine his light?

Your child looks up the underlined words in the dictionary and answers the questions.

Activities to Overcome a Poor Vocabulary

The vocabulary activities suggested in Chapter Four should help develop your child's vocabulary. In addition to those suggestions, the following activities can further increase your child's word power.

1. The next activity was developed by Joan Gipe to help children increase their vocabulary. Choose words from your child's science, math, or social studies textbooks that he may have difficulty understanding. For each selected word, write four different sentences using this same word. Let's look at an example.

   > It was *paramount* that John arrive on time for his sister's wedding. His sister's wedding was *paramount* to any of John's earlier plans. *Paramount* means to be of supreme or of chief importance. Can you tell of a situation that was *paramount* in your life?

   The first two sentences are to help your child understand the unknown word by using sentence meaning or the context. The third sentence defines the new word, and the last one asks your child to answer a question to check his understanding of the new word.

2. "Semantic Attribute Listing" can help expand your child's vocabulary and was developed by two leading reading experts, Dale Johnson and David Pearson. Choose a category like fishing and ask your child to write down words he associates with fishing. Give him three or four minutes to write down as many words as he can. Then ask him to explain how each of these

words is related to the general category. You may add some words associated with the category to develop his word knowledge. You may explain how you see different relationships among his identified words and the general category. This activity can help him understand how words are related to each other.

3. "Semantic Features Analysis," also developed by Johnson and Pearson, is another activity based on general categories. Select a category such as transportation. Ask your child to name different kinds of transportation. List these in a column on the left side of the paper. Ask your child to name some characteristics of transportation, such as wheels, steering, passengers, et cetera. Place these characteristics in a row along the top of the paper. It should look like the one shown below.

	Passengers	Wheels	Steering	Tires	Runners
rickshaw					
sled					
car					
unicycle					
truck					

Your child should decide how important the characteristic is to each kind of transportation. Use a number ranging from zero to five to indicate his answer. Zero means it's not necessary and a five indicates it's definitely needed. Numbers between zero and five indicate varying degrees of need. After your child has finished the grid, ask him to explain his decisions. Again, you may want to list additional types of transportation or characteristics to further expand his vocabulary.

4. Select topics from your child's subject area text-books and write each topic on an index card. On separate cards write one word that fits into one of the previously identified topics. Let your child place these word cards under the appropriate topic. An example is provided below.

Topic Cards

Birds	Fish	Rodent

Word Cards

cardinal	carp	squirrel
blue jay	salmon	rat
robin	trout	chipmunk
swallow	walleye	mouse

5. Ask your child to cut out advertisements using words or sentences to persuade people to buy a product. Your child should then replace the persuasive words with other emotionally-loaded words, making sure that the ad is still persuasive.

The activities suggested in the categories of comprehension, fluency, word identification, and vocabulary should help your child to overcome his reading difficulties. But, like any other skill, it takes a long time, lots of effort, and continual patience. Your child will not always be successful during his remedial reading program. He will experience both success and failure. He will seem to make progress and then appear to make his same old mistakes. Learning plateaus will occur, and you and your child may begin to think the goal will never be accomplished. But that is not so! With time, effort, and encouragement your child will succeed and become a proficient, skilled reader.

Why Do Reading Problems Occur?

A number of reasons cause children to have reading difficulties. To pinpoint a specific single cause is difficult, if not impossible. In most cases, children can compensate if it's a single problem. It is when there are several problems that children find it difficult to compensate, and reading breaks down. It is the old adage of "the straw that broke the camel's back." Let us consider the major causes for reading disabilities, which can be classified into four categories: physical, psychological, educational, and social-emotional.

Physical

Physical refers to the child's ability to see and hear normally. Print is clearly seen, and sounds are heard at low and high ranges. If a child can't see clearly or hear well, it can contribute to poor reading.

Psychological

The psychological category includes the ability to recognize visual and auditory differences in letters, words, and sounds. Intelligence and language are also a part of the psychological category. Intelligence includes the child's ability to develop concepts and understand relationships. It includes learning and remembering information. Language is also a part of this category and is quite important for reading development. Children need to have both speaking and listening abilities in English to develop reading skills. Understanding oral language is a basic requirement for learning to read; otherwise, learning to read is a slow and tedious process.

Educational

The educational category consists of methods, materials, and the teacher's ability to teach reading. A single method, single program, or a teacher's lack of knowledge can contribute to a child's reading problems. Children need to be taught by a variety of reading methods and materials. The teacher needs to be skillful at teaching reading. You, as a parent who has read and practiced the methods and activities suggested in this book, have developed a good understanding for teaching reading.

Social-Emotional

The last category, that of social-emotional factors, takes into account the family's values and beliefs and the emotional health of the child. The biases developed in the home can affect your child's learning either positively or negatively. If you believe it is not important for your child to learn how to read, your child will probably consider reading unimportant and will spend little effort in learning to read. If reading is important and an enjoyable activity in your home, the end result will most likely be that your child is a good reader. When too much pressure is placed on a child's reading achievement, it may cause him to avoid reading. He may have difficulty learning to read due to worry and fear of failure. Again, one single problem will probably not cause your child to experience reading difficulties. It is when many of these causes occur together that a child becomes a disabled reader.

Preventing Reading Problems

Your next question may be this one: "How can a parent prevent these reading problems?" Prevention may be accomplished in a number of ways. Regular physical examinations with your child's pediatrician and optometrist should identify any possible physical problems. The child who is nearsighted and doesn't realize he is not seeing as others normally do may become frustrated and avoid reading. If this child had been given an early visual examination, he probably would not have experienced frustration and given up on learning to read.

Listening, talking, and reading to your child each day develops your child's language skills and may prevent reading problems from ever occurring. Time spent on developing concepts and building a variety of experiences will diminish the likelihood of a reading disability. For example, cooking, gardening, hiking, fishing, etc. can help develop vocabulary and concepts required for skilled reading. These are all steps in preventing a problem in reading.

Most schools use a variety of methods and materials to teach reading. Make sure your child's school and teacher take this approach. Make an appointment with your child's teacher and find out how she teaches reading. If only one method (phonics, basal, or language experience) or set of materials is used, ask why. Discuss in a non-threatening manner some of the advantages for using a variety of methods and materials. Be careful not to put the teacher on the defensive.

Last but not least, when reading is a part of a family's leisure time, children grow to value reading. If reading is a family priority, it probably will become your child's priority. Sharing books with your child may be the best preventive measure of all.

Are There Differences Between Learning Disabilities and Reading Disabilities?

You may have heard about the learning disabled and wondered how these children differ from those who have reading problems. Children who are learning disabled (LD) have a number of other problems besides poor reading skills. Many times LD children are hyperactive. They are always moving and tend to be disruptive. Some have perceptual-motor problems in which they have difficulty copying letters from the blackboard. They often lack coordination and appear clumsy. A learning disabled child may be highly distractible and lack ability to concentrate on one thing for a long period of time. The LD child has been described as being impulsive. Remembering information and thinking about concepts often is difficult for this child. Usually these problems show up in reading, writing, and mathematics, and usually the LD child evidences more problems than just poor reading skills.

LD children may have all or several of the above difficulties, and they will vary in severity in each child. As a parent, you may notice your child seems to have many of these problems, but hasn't been diagnosed as LD. Don't assume your child is LD unless an educator has diagnosed him as such. If you do observe these characteristics in your child, tell your child's teacher and ask for a professional diagnosis. If he is LD, then the school is required by Public Law 94-142 to provide an appropriate education to meet his needs.

As mentioned earlier, the LD child often is a poor reader but has other problems beyond reading. Even though he has other difficulties, the LD child who is a poor reader can benefit from the reading activities suggested in this book.

What is Dyslexia?

Recently many magazines have published articles about dyslexia, warning parents about this major problem that prevents today's youth from learning to read. First of all, let's define dyslexia. Second, let's consider whether it is a major problem.

Webster's dictionary defines it as "a disturbance of the ability to read." Others have linked it to brain damage, affecting children's ability to see letters and words as normal individuals do. Supposedly, letters and words appear reversed or upside down. But no one can be totally sure how the child with dyslexia actually sees words. Still others label any poor reader dyslexic. Since there is confusion and lack of agreement over the definition of dyslexia, many educators and psychologists don't use this term. Because agreement on a definition for dyslexia can't be reached, it is virtually impossible to identify the number of children exhibiting this problem.

Whether or not a child can be considered dyslexic is not the major concern. Putting a label on a child who can't read isn't helping him to overcome the problem or providing any further insight in developing more effective reading instruction. The poor reader, dyslexic or not, can benefit from the type of instruction suggested in this book.

Suggestions for Parents

1. Disabled readers need a great deal of recreational reading to overcome their difficulties. Take your child to the library or book store to select books he is interested in reading. Joining book clubs in school may be another opportunity for choosing interesting books. Magazines can also provide needed reading practice. Try to obtain some high-interest, low-vocabulary books. These books are simpler to read than many of the typical library books. Even though they are easier to read, the topics are of interest to an older child.

2. Commercial crossword puzzle books are good for increasing word power. Choose those which are designed for children.

3. Disabled readers many times have difficulties using a dictionary. One of the following dictionaries may be easier for your child to use.

   a) *Macmillan Dictionary for Children*
   b) *Webster's First Dictionary*
   c) *My First Dictionary*—American Heritage

Chapter 8

MEETING THE NEEDS of the GIFTED CHILD

Sitting at a computer terminal busily designing a computer program is seven-year-old Steve. Steve was five when he first became interested in computers. At the early age of three, Steve taught himself to read and enjoyed reading picture books to his baby sitter. At age five, Steve not only understood cause and effect situations, but could easily explain why these situations occurred. A typical conversation for Steve would be explaining to a five-year-old playmate that anyone who turns too sharply on the loose gravel in the driveway will fall from his bicycle. When he was six, Steve could not only add and subtract, but was also beginning to multiply and divide. He learned each of these skills quickly, easily, and well before most children his age. Not only does Steve have superb ability, but his ideas are creative. He is motivated to try new things and always finishes projects he begins. It is no surprise that Steve is considered a gifted youngster. He has many of the characteristics of giftedness. He is bright, high achieving, creative, and motivated to finish projects. There are not many gifted children like Steve. In fact, it is estimated that three to five percent of the school population can be considered gifted.

Who Is Gifted?

What does it mean to be gifted? If your child is gifted, is he talented in all areas, such as science, mathematics, and art? Does he have an extraordinarily high IQ of 130 or above? Is he bored with school and does he tend to think he is superior to others? Is he a bookworm with narrow interests? Or is he a high achiever, always getting A's in school? Many of these questions don't have simple, straightforward answers. For example, the first question — "What does it mean to be gifted?" — doesn't have a clear-cut answer. There is no universal definition of giftedness. There are many definitions that are continually debated among educators, psychologists, and parents. The federal government has established its own definition, but this lacks specific standards that schools and parents can use to accurately identify a gifted youngster.

Let's look at the federal guidelines for identifying and educating the gifted.

> Gifted and talented children means children, and whenever applicable, youth, who are identified at the preschool, elementary, or secondary level as possessing demonstrated or potential abilities that give evidence of high performance capability in areas such as intellectual, creative, specific academic, or leadership ability, or in the performing and visual arts, and who by reason thereof require services or activities not ordinarily provided by the school.

Do you notice there are a number of unclear ideas in the federal definition? Consider the phrase "high performance capability." Does this mean receiving A's in all subject areas, or does it mean receiving high test scores? Much has been left to interpretation, and those most often interpreting giftedness are teachers who apply an individual school district's guidelines.

Originally, to be considered gifted, an individual had to have an IQ of 130 or above. After considerable research, educators and psychologists are questioning the sole use of IQ testing for identifying a gifted child and believe it is a narrow and limited way to identify giftedness. Many gifted individuals don't have an IQ of even close to 130, but they are incredibly creative and successful. In the past, schools placed too much emphasis on the IQ test and overlooked many gifted youngsters. Happily, now schools are using a variety of informational sources to identify gifted children and have also lowered the IQ score requirement.

If gifted doesn't mean an individual with a high IQ, then what characteristics can be associated with giftedness? Here are a few: Gifted individuals tend to exhibit leadership qualities. They often achieve excellent grades and score high on achievement tests. Many have an exceptional memory and are good at problem-solving. Often the gifted are quite creative and, for example, can develop new uses for common objects. Some are talented in art, music, and athletics. Most have broad interests and have knowledge on a number of subjects. You'll notice that gifted children have long attention spans and stick-to-itiveness. Projects are completed and done well. The gifted are usually extremely curious and ask so many questions, parents and teachers can become weary.

Not all of these characteristics describe each gifted youngster but can assist you in correctly identifying your child as gifted.

It is important to identify giftedness early so that the child will receive an appropriate education. Too often gifted children are overlooked and become behavior problems in school because they aren't sufficiently challenged and stimulated. Inappropriate behavior, once developed, is difficult to change. Sadly, some who haven't been identified as gifted have settled into mediocrity, merely receiving passing grades and average test scores. If not challenged, gifted children become bored with school.

Each school has its own standards for identifying gifted children. Call your child's school and ask how they identify children for placement in gifted programs. Many schools are using IQ scores, achievement scores, and teacher and parent recommendations to better identify gifted children.

Carefully review the school's approach in selecting the gifted. Make sure IQ scores aren't the number one priority. Remember, this is only one indicator and not the most important. Check if the IQ test is given to groups or individually. The most valid would be an individual IQ test given by a school psychologist. Also, ask for the specific points teachers have been instructed to consider for recommending a child to a gifted program.

If your child seems to possess most of the characteristics we've discussed and has high abilities, creative talents, and motivation, contact your child's teacher and discuss your observations. The earlier your child is identified, the more likely he will receive appropriate instruction to better develop his talents and reach his potential.

Instructional Needs of the Gifted

Once your child has been identified as gifted, what specific services should the school provide? Should specific kinds of instruction be presented? Are there guidelines for evaluating the school's gifted reading program?

The School's Responsibility to the Gifted

Federal laws and legislation have not mandated special education for the gifted. However, some states do require such educational opportunities. It has been argued that if gifted children don't receive an appropriate education, it can't be assumed that they will reach their full potential. However, studies to date have not supported the effectiveness of gifted programs, making federal legislation and funding for gifted education difficult to acquire.

Even though the federal government doesn't mandate special education for the gifted, many schools have provided special educational opportunities for these exceptional children. Such educational opportunities vary widely — from field trips to special schools and programs. Some schools offer summer institutes especially designed for the gifted. Other schools hire special teachers to teach gifted youngsters. Independent study, accelerated classes, and special projects are other ways schools have tried to meet the needs of the gifted child.

Some schools have special reading programs for the gifted. Let's take a look at some gifted reading programs for the primary-aged child (ages 5-8), the intermediate-aged child (ages 9-10), and the adolescent (ages 11-13) as described by Barbe, Renzulli, Labuda, and Callahan.

A literature club is the basis of one such primary gifted program in which general reading skills are continually developed with emphasis on creativity, evaluation, and leadership. During each club meeting, different children serve as group discussion leaders. Within these meetings, all children evaluate their individual progress as well as the group's progress.

For the intermediate-aged gifted child, another type of literature program is available. This program focuses on fiction and poetry. Children develop insights into human behavior by recognizing how the environment influences the motives and behaviors of human beings. Activities require children to sequence events in a story, analyze characters' motives, and interpret the mood, theme, and author's purpose.

Problem-solving, along with practical application, is the core of an excellent adolescent gifted program. Gifted students first receive instruction in the process of problem-solving by learning a number of techniques. One technique is brainstorming, which encourages immediate development of ideas with no concern for critical analysis. Another technique, called attribute listing, requires the identification of physical characteristics and purposes of objects in order to make improvements. The problem-solving course is followed by the presentation of a number of problematic situations. The adolescent is expected to apply problem-solving techniques to reach a solution to these everyday problems.

Is your gifted child participating in a similar kind of special reading program? If not, why not? Discuss with your child's teacher or principal the gifted reading program the school offers. If one doesn't exist, you should discuss the possibility of initiating one. This may be a good opportunity for members of the local parent-teacher organization to volunteer their services. Sources for establishing gifted programs are included in the section "Suggestions for Parents" on page 204.

As you talk to your child's teacher or principal about the school's current gifted reading program, you may want to use the following questions.

1. Does the teacher provide unique and challenging reading activities especially designed for the gifted?

2. Does the gifted reading program include activities to broaden your child's knowledge and interests?

3. Does the gifted reading program include stimulating reading and other activities to encourage interest and reading enjoyment?

4. Does your gifted child help plan and organize some of his own reading activities?

5. Does your child's teacher concentrate on developing abstract and critical thinking?

6. Does the teacher key some activities to your child's interests?

7. Are there books and magazines in your child's classroom to match his high reading level?

8. Is the teacher trained and experienced in teaching reading to gifted youngsters?

9. Does the teacher encourage questioning and exploring of topics?

10. Are there only a few activities that "drill" low level reading skills?

Each question may not receive an immediate "yes" answer, but you want your child's school to continue to strive to develop an effective gifted reading program. The above questions focus on five major areas important to gifted education. They are: individualization, high level thinking, individual interests, variety of reading materials, and reading appreciation. Let's take a closer look at these five important areas in a gifted reading program. You will want to discuss these areas with your child's teacher to make sure your child is receiving a quality gifted reading program.

Individualization

The gifted child benefits from an individualized reading program geared to his interests and abilities that he helps to plan and organize. To keep motivation high, the gifted child needs to have challenging activities that continually increase his knowledge. Too much of the drill and repetition needed for the average learner will quickly become boring to the fast-paced learning style of the gifted child. Challenging instruction allows the young gifted child to continually develop and apply his ability. It reduces the chance of disinterest and boredom due to inappropriate teaching.

High Level Thinking

In any gifted program, the child should be given opportunities to apply new learnings. For example, he might not only learn about what archaeologists do, but become an archaeologist and go on an actual dig. Such projects require the gifted child to think at a variety of levels. Other examples include surveying plots of land after learning trigonometry concepts, learning about cinematography and then writing and producing a movie. These projects may sound complicated, but gifted children are involved in just such projects throughout the country.

But beyond practical and immediate application, the gifted child should be asked to analyze, synthesize, and evaluate. All levels of thinking are important for all children to develop, but the gifted child learns such levels earlier and faster with finer detail and greater depth, with less structure, and more independence.

Learning about Individual Interests

Most gifted children have developed a variety of interests before they enter school. It is the teacher's responsibility to find out the interests of each gifted youngster so an effective individualized program can be developed. She can use a variety of techniques to find out your child's interests. She can talk to you or your child, observe his selection of free reading materials, and give him an informal "interest" survey specifically designed to learn not only his interests but also how much he already knows about them. Basing reading instruction on your gifted child's interests will greatly increase his motivation and learning.

Variety of Reading Materials

The typical school reading program uses a single textbook that probably includes a variety of approaches for teaching reading. The practice of using children's literature to teach reading skills is not commonplace. Children's literature is used for enjoyment and for practice of reading skills, but it isn't typically used to teach reading. Gifted students will not be challenged by a textbook program intended for average readers. Not only will learning be inhibited, but the gifted child will probably find such a program uninteresting and boring.

A vast assortment of materials is necessary for a gifted reading program if individualization is to be accomplished and interests are to be met. Without numerous materials, the program may become ineffective and dull. Materials cost money, and schools are usually short of funds. Therefore, schools generally appreciate book donations or parent-teacher organization fundraisers for purchasing additional children's literature.

Appreciation of Reading

It can't be emphasized too greatly that teachers need to develop an appreciation for reading in *all* children. But it is especially important for the gifted since these children are to be the innovators and leaders of the future.

It has been said that we need bright children who will be capable of making the world a better place in the future. If we believe this, then the schools need to be concerned about providing an appropriate education for gifted children. Their potential and the future of the world may depend on it.

The Parents' Role in Fostering Learning

There are many ways you can contribute to the development of your gifted child. One way is to provide an enriched environment. For your preschooler, a trip to the zoo, a walk in the woods, a visit to a children's museum, library, theater, and other exciting places encourage language growth, develop concepts, and broaden experiences.

For example, a trip to the zoo gives you and your child the opportunity to identify different animals, to discuss the variety of ways in which they live, and to compare their physical appearances. This kind of discussion teaches new vocabulary, stimulates thinking, and increases your child's knowledge of animals. The gifted young child can grasp ideas quicker and is able to understand more abstract ideas than other children the same age. If your child is interested and enjoying himself, don't be afraid to use difficult words and to discuss complex concepts. Gifted children need to be involved in a stimulating environment.

As your child matures and develops his own specific interests and hobbies, you will need to provide him with additional information and advanced experiences related to those personal interests. The child who enjoys writing books would probably find it fascinating to meet children's authors and talk to them about their choices of topics, characters, plots, et cetera. Children can meet authors at special events, at libraries, or at bookstores. The older gifted child is apt to seek out additional information on his own rather than relying on adults. At this important stage of development, parents really need to encourage and provide opportunities for their gifted child to continually acquire knowledge.

Besides enriched surroundings, the gifted child also benefits from discussions with adults. Both younger and older gifted youngsters will increase their vocabulary and creative thinking ability when parents discuss a variety of topics. For example, younger children can learn from a discussion in which new uses for a broomstick handle, spoon, hand mixer, or other household objects are contemplated. Frequent discussions like these can increase your child's creative thinking skills.

The older child may enjoy reading about domestic problems in our country, discussing what has been done in the past as well as possible solutions. A relevant problem to read and discuss is the use of nuclear energy for electricity. What are the problems associated with nuclear energy? Are there alternative ways to make electricity? Are they as practical and efficient? How can we make sure electricity is produced safely and inexpensively? This kind of topic is a good way to develop problem-solving skills.

You will find that gifted children tend to have a lot of questions. The best thing parents can do is answer their questions honestly. If you don't know the answer, you can look it up together. Don't be afraid that your answers may be too complex. The gifted child is able to understand abstract and complicated ideas and does not particularly appreciate a simple response.

You and your child may enjoy asking each other questions about his special interest. Exchanging questions can be a motivating and challenging activity. As you continually spend time discussing various topics with your child, you will find that his interests will broaden, his abilities will increase, and his curiosities will enlarge. Much of these results are due to the amount and quality of your discussions. You will find your time well spent.

Instilling confidence is beneficial to all children's growth and happiness. And it is definitely important to develop in the gifted. Even though the gifted are intelligent and able, they still need their parents' interest and confidence. The gifted child is "different" from his peers, and may often feel uncomfortable and concerned about how others perceive him. Therefore, it is important that parents encourage, praise, and wholeheartedly approve of their child's ideas and accomplishments. Parents can do wonders for developing a child's self-confidence and establishing a positive self-concept. If a child has confidence and feels good about himself, he will not be concerned about being different or unique. Begin to develop your child's self-confidence at an early age and nourish it throughout his childhood. Your child will develop a positive and healthy mental attitude that can only help him to succeed.

Don't encourage your child constantly to seek perfection. Gifted children tend to be perfectionists and have high expectations of themselves. They place a great deal of pressure to succeed on themselves. They may even fear failure. As a parent, you can help your gifted youngster better understand human weaknesses. Discuss some of the following ideas: There is no such thing as perfection. All people regularly experience failure. Making mistakes is part of everyday life. We can learn from failure. Discussions such as this can increase your child's self-understanding and help build his self-confidence.

A place for exploration and experimentation is necessary for your gifted child to continually develop and learn. As a parent, you are in the best position to provide your child with such a place. The perfect place is one where your child need not worry about ruining a carpet, table top, or creating a mess. This doesn't mean that your child is never asked to straighten and organize his room. It does mean that he needs the freedom to explore, experiment, and create without repercussions.

What kind of environment encourages a gifted child to experiment, explore, and create? Your child needs an area large enough to have a table and chairs of a comfortable height. Inexpensive shelves or cabinets are handy to hold materials and projects. The floor should be tile or cement so it can be easily cleaned. Create an area in which your child can easily try experiments and projects without fearing he'll ruin or damage it. Next, your child needs materials to experiment and explore. Everyday objects and materials found in your home usually invite his curiosity. Here is a list of suggested materials for gifted children ages two through thirteen. You may select from this list those items which seem best suited to your child's interests, development, and abilities.

Materials for the Gifted Child

1. clay
2. pencils, pens, crayons, chalk, craypas, paint brushes
3. paper (unlined and lined), art tissue, colored construction paper, cardboard, poster board
4. paint
5. chalkboard
6. table, chairs, desk, old sofa, old rug, beanbag chair, etc.
7. bookshelves
8. magazines, newspapers, fiction and nonfiction books, poetry, comic books
9. cloth remnants

10. paper punch, scissors, stapler
11. glue or paste
12. all types of containers
13. string, rope
14. wood
15. nails
16. scraps of metal and wire
17. batteries
18. empty spools of thread
19. plants and seeds
20. blocks or other building devices
21. drinking straws or plastic tubing
22. ruler, compass
23. magnets
24. old clothes for dress up
25. buttons, beads
26. tape recorder, blank tapes
27. puppet theater
28. socks
29. chemistry set
30. cash register, paper money, and coins
31. magnifying glass

Other items could be included, but the ones listed will allow your child to enter into the magical world of creativity. But do not hesitate to provide additional objects and materials as required.

Besides designing an interesting environment for your gifted child, try some joint activities. The activities suggested below are specifically focused on the child who is gifted in reading and the other areas of language (writing, speaking, and listening). You can adapt the suggested activities to the needs of your child. Have fun learning together!

1. The gifted child is often an avid reader and reads voraciously about his interests. His enthusiastic reading habits should be encouraged. But, in addition, this young reader needs to be introduced to new and different topics so that he will acquire new interests. As a parent, you can do this easily by taking your child to the library and exploring the variety of reading materials available there, such as fiction, nonfiction, poetry, and magazines. Sit down together and share these materials by reading to him or letting him read to you. Discuss what you are learning together and don't be afraid to use complex vocabulary and sentence structure. More than likely he will understand, and difficult material stimulates growth. Encourage him to ask questions as well as pose questions to him at a variety of levels. Ask a few factual questions, but concentrate on questions that require him to interpret and apply the author's ideas. Your gifted child also needs to answer those questions that call for alternative solutions to problems or create new ways to use an object. Focus on questions like the following:

- What other ways could the character have solved the problem?
- How else could the main character react to his father's accident?
- Has anything like this happened to you? How did you feel? Why did you feel this way?
- Would you have done the same thing this character did in the story? Why or why not?
- In your opinion, did the character handle the problem well? Why or why not?

2. Encourage your gifted youngster to pose questions to which he wants answers. These questions may range from easy to complex, and some may even be unanswerable. All questions are important if they are valuable to the learner. Encourage your child to use books to seek answers. Suggest that he write down his question and answer, and then discuss his findings. Searching for answers may be done together or your child may prefer doing it himself.

3. The Creative Thinking-Reading Activity (CT-RA) developed by Martha Haggard stimulates divergent thinking. Choose a fiction story your child has read and enjoyed. Eliminate an important event in the story and ask your child how this might affect the outcome of the story. Suggest that he describe orally or in writing how the story would conclude. Remove major characters or change the time and place of the story and ask your child to write a story without this selected story element.

4. After devouring many books on a specific interest or hobby, suggest to your child that he write an informative book for his friends. After the book is written, suggest that he illustrate and bind it. Now the book is ready for sharing.

5. Choose a complex book in an area of your child's interest to read and discuss together. Discuss the book in light of possible gaps in his knowledge. Talk about the unsolved problems the author presents. Exchange views about other possibilities that could occur, but were not discussed by the author.

6. After reading folk and fairy tales, you and your child may find it interesting to write a modern, contemporary version of the tale. The second or third time you do this, your child may enjoy writing it alone. A good tale to rewrite is

Cinderella based on the thoughts and values of today's modern woman.

7. Write unique newspaper or magazine ads for household objects.

8. Select books that use figurative language, such as simile, metaphor, personification, et cetera. Read and discuss how figurative language affects the meaning of the story.

9. Many gifted children are extremely curious and wonder how things work. Books that invite children to experiment can broaden your child's knowledge. Here are some good books with which to start.

   Goldstein-Jackson, K., Rudnick, N.E., Human, R. *Experiments With Everyday Objects.* Englewood Cliffs, NJ: Prentice-Hall, 1978.

   Stein, S. *The Science Book.* New York: Workman Publishing, 1979.

   Kohl, H. *A Book of Puzzlements.* New York: Schocken Books, 1981.

   Jacobson, W.J., Bergman, A.B. *Science Activities for Children.* Englewood Cliffs, NJ: Prentice-Hall, 1983.

10. If your child writes unique and enjoyable stories or poems, he may want to try to have them published. Here are a few places that consider children's work:

    Ebony Jr.
    820 S. Michigan Avenue
    Chicago, IL 60605

    Highlights for Children
    803 Church Street
    Honesdale, PA 18431

Young World
The Saturday Evening Post Co.
Youth Division
P.O. Box 567B
Indianapolis, IN 46206

Child Life
P.O. Box 567B
Indianapolis, IN 46206

Stone Soup
P.O. Box 33
Santa Cruz, CA 95063

Current Consumer
Curriculum Innovations, Inc.
501 Lake Forest Avenue
Highland Park, IL 60040

Wombat
365 Ashton Drive
Athens, GA 30600

Jack and Jill
P.O. Box 567
Indianapolis, IN 46206

Electric Company Magazine
P.O. Box 2926
Boulder, CO 80322

Cricket League
P.O. Box 100
LaSalle, IL 61301

Write a letter of inquiry before your child sends any original pieces. Each magazine has specific guidelines that need to be followed. Some have yearly contests for art, poetry, riddles, jokes, and stories. Ask for rules and deadlines. Letters about specific articles that have already appeared in the magazine are also accepted by many of the above publishers.

11. Your gifted child may enjoy researching the plants or vegetables that grow best in your home region. After he completes his research, suggest he design a garden using those plants or vegetables.

12. Interviewing various family members for a family history may be fun for your gifted child. He will need first to plan the topics and questions to be covered in his family history. Not only will personal or telephone interviews be planned but letters may need to be written for those who live far away. Once he has his information, he can begin to write. The entire family will enjoy reading about its roots.

13. Your child may enjoy developing his own word games for others to enjoy. Designing crossword puzzles, word searches, codes, riddles, etc. can be an enjoyable learning experience.

14. Your gifted child may enjoy setting up his own business. He can read about and develop a new kind of toy or novelty for children. What a great way to learn business skills!

15. Suggest to your child that he write his own puppet play and perform it before family and friends.

16. Encourage your child to keep a journal of what he sees and observes each day. He will begin to develop insights about our complex world.

17. Scamper is an enjoyable game developed by Robert Eberle. Each letter stands for a different step in the game. Let's try an example to learn the different steps.

    Substitute: If you needed a can opener but didn't have one, what could you use in its place?
    Combine: What can you make with a can opener, a can, and a bottle?

Adapt: How could you change the can opener so your dog could open his own dog food?

Modify or make larger or smaller: How could you make a can opener small enough to fit a 3" x 3" area?

Put to other uses: What else could you use a can opener for besides opening cans?

Eliminate: What would happen if there were no handle on the can opener?

Reverse or rearrange: How would you use a can opener if it opened cans from the bottom rather than the top?

Suggestions to Parents

1. For further information about the gifted, consult these books, magazines, and organizations:

   Labuda, M (Ed.) *Creative Reading for Gifted Learners: A Design for Excellence.* Newark, DE: International Reading Association, 1974.

   Polette, N. & Hamlin, M. *Exploring Books with Gifted Children.* Littleton, CO: Libraries Unlimited, 1980.

   Witty, P. (Ed.) *Reading for the Gifted and the Creative Student.* Newark, DE: International Reading Association, 1971.

   Ginsberg, G. & Harrison, C.H. *How to Help Your Gifted Child: A Handbook for Parents and Teachers.* New York: Monarch Press, 1977.

   Gifted Children Newsletter
   1255 Portland Place
   P.O. Box 2581
   Boulder, CO 80322

   Gifted Child Quarterly
   National Association for Gifted Children
   217 Gregory Drive
   Hot Springs, AR 71901

   International Reading Association
   Gifted Chapter
   Box 8139, Barksdale Road
   Newark, DE 19711

National Association for Gifted Children
217 Gregory Drive
Hot Springs, AR 71901

2. Gifted children need to read books which challenge them. To provide your child with exceptional books, you may find this resource book helpful: Baskin, B.H. & Harris, K.H. *Books for the Gifted Child*. New York, NY: R.R. Bowker, 1980.

3. Your child may be experiencing some difficulties because he's gifted. A good book for him to read is *The Gifted Kids' Survival Guide* by Judy Galbraith and published by Wetherall.

"ONE HUNDRED COPIES, PLEASE."

Chapter 9

COMPUTERS CAN HELP

If you look at any newspaper or magazine, you will notice the numerous ads about computers. Most are about personal computers suitable for home and office use. All extol the virtues of ease in using. We hear such phrases as "computer friendly" and "user friendly."

Recent books such as *The Third Wave* and *Megatrends* claim that we are an information society and no longer an industrial society. We must equip ourselves and our children to meet the needs of this information explosion. The only way to meet the challenge of the future is to become computer literate. John Naisbitt in *Megatrends* predicts that by 1985 three-fourths of all jobs will involve computers. Such forecasts have led parent task forces and school boards to get on the bandwagon and demand that computer education become a part of the school curriculum.

If we look around our world, we see that most everything is computerized — from calculators to ordinary household gadgets. Our community is computerized. In libraries, we no longer look up books manually in the card catalog; instead we use a computer terminal. Stores use computerized cash registers, and we receive a detailed printout of each item purchased. We are definitely in the midst of the computer age.

Unfortunately, the media attempts to make parents feel that they are depriving their children of learning and future success if a family doesn't have its own computer. As a parent, you've probably felt this pressure from reading and hearing headlines such as "Give Your Child a Head Start" (referring to owning a computer system). On the other hand, you're probably also hearing child psychologists describe the ills of the hurried child who is expected to learn and do things earlier than ever before, thus losing many of the joys of childhood.

As a parent, what should you do? The old adage "Too much of anything is bad" holds true. Encouraging your child to master and use a computer can be beneficial as well as fun if you use common sense. As has been emphasized throughout this book, once your child becomes anxious or disinterested, stop the activity and do something else. You can't help your child if his attention isn't focused on the activity. In fact, pushing him to continue can promote a bad attitude towards learning, and that is certainly not the end result you wish to create. Of course, you want your child to enjoy growing up, but you really need not worry about "pushing" him to achieve. Just observe his attitude and behaviors which will quickly let you know when the learning activity should be stopped for that day. Closely observing your child's needs will ensure he'll learn but continue to enjoy his childhood.

Computer Basics

Do you have to be a computer expert to help your child learn about computers? No, together you can easily learn computer skills. How can you learn to use a computer without going through time and expense to purchase a computer system? It's not as convenient as sitting down in front of your own computer, but libraries now make computers available for patrons. Schools and local community colleges offer classes in different computers, software programs, and various computer languages. Often this is the ideal way to get your feet wet. You don't invest much money, and you become acquainted with a variety of computers. As a result, you become better able to choose the right computer system for your family.

Hardware

The personal computer is the prevalent system found in homes and schools. A personal computer system is made up of two major elements: hardware and software. What do we mean by computer hardware? The central processing unit or CPU, memory, storage devices, and input/output devices make up the hardware of a computer system.

The CPU is housed in a covered unit on which the keyboard is found. In a personal computer, the CPU is a small chip, a little more than a centimeter square. This chip is quite remarkable. It carries out the functions of the computer. It is, indeed, the brain of the computer.

The CPU is designed to receive commands from a user, for example, your child. It then can carry out the command, provide the requested information, and store this information. What a nifty tool! Even more extraordinary, this little microchip never makes mistakes, and it completes tasks at an incredible speed far superior to human capabilities.

The CPU doesn't use the English language to communicate. It uses a binary system of zeros and ones to carry out commands. However, we don't communicate with the computer using the binary system; rather we use a different language to translate our commands. You probably have heard of Fortran, Cobol, and Basic, which are some of the more popular and simple computer languages. But these languages take time to learn. However, with the advances of computer programming, many people don't even need to learn these languages to use a computer. You and your child will be able to use programs that don't require knowledge of a computer language. Application programs, as they are called, allow for easy and simple communication between you and the computer. Often you'll hear these programs referred to as "user friendly." Most of the programs we'll discuss don't require any programming language but use the English language, and each is simple and easy to run.

Now let's turn our attention to another hardware component—memory. What is memory? Memory gives the CPU workspace to carry out the commands given by your child. There are two kinds of memory. One kind is called "Read Only Memory" or ROM. As its name indicates, ROM reads directions permanently programmed by the manufacturer. These directions are repeatedly used by the computer and allow your child to use more complicated and powerful programs.

The second kind of memory is called "Random Access Memory" or RAM. Its function is to provide workspace for the tasks your child wants it to accomplish. For example, if your child is composing a story, RAM provides your child space to write his story as well as make changes. But RAM's memory can be very unstable! I'm sure you've heard of someone "losing" his project when the computer is mistakenly turned off or the electrical power goes off. Once the computer is shut off, your work is gone unless it is stored. This leads us to the next component—storage devices.

An important part of the computer system is storage—a place to save your work so you will always have it. There are a variety of storage devices. Tape recorder, hard disc, and floppy discs are the storage systems used for personal computers. The tape recorder is the same cassette recorder you use to listen to music except there is a special connector needed to convert audio signals to the digital kind used by computers. Your child can learn to use the cassette player with a computer in the same manner as he records and plays music. However, cassette players are not frequently used since they are slow and unreliable, and it is hard to locate previously stored work on them.

The most popular storage device is the floppy disc. The floppy disc looks like a miniature record. It fits into a machine called a disc drive that is connected to the computer. The disc acts like a tape. It records your child's work and allows your child to "call it up" on the computer. The floppy disc is relatively fast, efficient, and affordable.

The hard disc works like a floppy disc, but it has much greater storage capacity and is much faster. With greater speed and more space, the cost is also greater. In most cases, your child's needs won't require this more expensive storage system. Floppy discs will probably meet your family's needs.

The last component of computer hardware is the input and output devices. The input devices your child will normally use in school will be a keyboard similar to that of a typewriter, a light pen, a joy stick, or game paddles. These devices allow your child to put information into the computer. If your child wants to write a story, he uses the keyboard. If your child is engaged in a reading activity, he may use only a few keys on the keyboard. To play games, he may use game paddles or a joy stick. Game paddles or joy sticks consist of a box with a movable stick. The stick can be moved in all directions to move objects on the computer screen. Your young child will find joy sticks or game paddles much easier to use than the normal keyboard. A light pen is also used to put or change information in the computer. By touching the light pen against the surface of the screen, information changes. The light pen is easy to use but can be more unreliable than game paddles and the keyboard.

Output devices make it possible to see the information you have put into the computer. The two output devices usually found in school and home computers are a TV screen or what is often called a CRT and a printer. For more technical information about computers, check out those books recommended in the section at the end of this chapter, "Suggestions to Parents."

Software

A computer is useless without software. Software informs the computer what to do so that your child, for example, can use a word processing program to write his story. The software programs contain the instructions or commands to make the computer system function. Now that you know a little about the computer system, how can it help your child with learning? Specifically, how can it help your child to read? Programming, computer assisted instruction, and word processing are three different ways in which computers can increase your child's learning. Let's consider each separately.

Making the Computer Work!

Programming: Children's Style

Can you think of anything more exciting and challenging than for your child to design instructions for the computer to complete a task? Your child is in control of the computer. This is what programming is all about. The two most popular programming languages for children are BASIC and Logo. These two languages offer your child the opportunity to learn to think in logical terms. Logo also has other benefits such as exploring geometric concepts using graphics. Programming seems to help improve reading skills, and because it encourages logical thinking, programming can help a child also to think in logical terms while reading.

BASIC requires your child to break a task down into simple sequential steps. Your child writes a set of explicit directions to accomplish the task he wants to create. For example, one of the first programs children usually learn is to instruct the computer to say hello and print their name. To do this, your child has to reason what the first step is, followed by the second step, and continuing until the computer can correctly run his program.

Here are some books that will provide more information about BASIC:

Galanter, E. *Kids and Computers*. New York: Perigee Books, 1983.

Lipscomb, S.D. & Zuanich, M. *Basic Beginnings*. New York: Avon Books, 1983.

Lampton, C. *Programming in Basic*. New York: Franklin Watts, 1983.

Harris, D. & Harris, P. *Computer Programming 1, 2, 3!* New York: Grosset & Dunlap, 1983.

As a parent, you'll find the first book listed particularly helpful. Galanter not only teaches your child how to program with BASIC, but he also explains computers to parents. The second book is for both you and your child to explore the programming language of BASIC. It includes hints on helping your child learn about computers. Don't worry if you know almost nothing about BASIC. This book is designed for you and your child to learn together in your pleasant, quiet home atmosphere. The last two books can help your child learn how to program with BASIC.

The second popular computer language is Logo developed by Seymour Papert and others at the Massachusetts Institute of Technology. The original purpose in developing Logo was to create opportunities for children to explore computers and geometric principles. Because Papert believes effective learning can be accomplished by the computer, Logo was developed. It is based on the idea that children learn concepts by exploring and discovering the world for themselves.

Logo is quite different from BASIC. This language is concerned only with graphics. The graphics created by Logo are better known as "turtle graphics." In Logo, the child uses English commands to instruct the turtle to move according to mathematical concepts. Through turtle graphics, your child explores geometric concepts, such as angles, squares, and triangles. Logo, like BASIC, helps your child think logically. And isn't logical thinking necessary in order to apply and evaluate what one reads? Logo is available for most personal computers. Most personal computers also accept BASIC without additional software. But, if not, you can purchase a BASIC interpreter in software.

Computer Assisted Instruction

Computer assisted instruction or CAI for short is quite different from programming. With CAI, you and your child don't need to know a computer language. Most CAI programs are considered "user friendly." They have simple directions and for the most part are foolproof to operate. Basically, all one needs to know is how to turn the computer on and off although it's helpful to use an introductory program presenting the basics of computer operation. For example, to become familiar with the Apple computer, start by using the introductory software program "Apple Presents Apple." This will save time when using future software programs on the Apple computer. Most computer manufacturers have a software program that explains the general operations of their computer.

What is CAI and how can it help your child with reading? CAI is considered a tool to help children accomplish specific goals by using traditional educational methods presented on a computer. CAI programs can be placed into several different categories: drill and practice, tutorials, simulations, instructional games, and demonstrations.

Drill and practice has been critically referred to as the "electronic workbook page." It emphasizes a specific reading skill, such as recognizing the "ch" sound in the word "children" and repeats this idea over and over until the child knows it automatically. In a typical drill and practice program, the child may be asked to press the "y" key for "yes" or the "n" key for "no" to identify whether the "ch" sound is heard in the word "chin." This same idea is repeated until the child knows the sound well.

Many times a quiz is given to check the child's ability to use the skill being taught.

Drill and practice programs have received much criticism since paper and pencil exercises can easily accomplish the same task and with much less expense. Many educators feel that computers can be put to better use through programming, simulations, and word processing. There is, however, some value to drill and practice programs. Unlike most paper and pencil exercises, drill and practice programs provide immediate feedback. Your child knows at once if his response is correct or incorrect. He doesn't keep reinforcing incorrect learning. Children usually aren't enthusiastic about drill and practice exercises, but there is an exception—if drill and practice is done by computer, most children are motivated and enjoy it. The machine aspect of a computer is intriguing to children. They are in control of the machine. Usually there are graphics and sound associated with each program that make it inviting. Correct responses are rewarded to make children feel good about themselves. Incorrect responses usually receive encouragement rather than criticism. It is a fact that in order to learn, some drill and practice is needed, so why not use a tool like the computer to make it more interesting?

Many of the programs found in computer stores are of the drill and practice variety, and some drill and practice programs are better than others. Be a critical consumer! Later in this chapter, a list of criteria to use when purchasing software will be presented

Tutorials are another category of CAI programs. In tutorials, the computer plays the role of teacher. The computer presents information after which questions are asked that check the child's understanding. For example, a tutorial may teach how to select the main idea of a paragraph by explaining that the main idea may often be found in the first or last sentence of a paragraph. The computer then may use paragraphs to illustrate this explanation. To check the child's understanding, several paragraphs may be presented that ask him to select the main idea from several choices.

Many educators have also criticized tutorials because these programs accept only one answer as correct. In reading and understanding text, many times there are many acceptable answers to a question, depending on the reader's experiences and prior knowledge. Thus, tutorials may limit your child's thinking while reading. This is a valid criticism. Too much of this kind of teaching may cause misconceptions about reading comprehension. If there is always only one acceptable answer, the program's quality and value is lessened.

However, there are some good tutorials such as "Story Tree" published by Scholastic. In this program, for children aged nine through twelve, your child learns how to write an acceptable story.

Simulations are another category of CAI programs. Unlike drill and practice and tutorials, simulations appear to be the most promising computer programs of the future. At present there are far more drill and practice and tutorials than simulations. As the name indicates, simulations reenact real life experiences so your child develops some expertise without taking any risks. For example, computer simulations are commonly used to train or update airplane pilots. Dangerous situations during flight are designed so that if this situation actually does occur, the pilot automatically knows what to do. Also, drivers' training programs often use computer simulations.

Besides their obvious benefit in training programs, simulation programs are being developed to teach reading skills. Problem-solving is one reading skill in which simulation programs can be quite helpful. "Who Stole Cinderella's Slipper?" (published by Book Lures, Inc.) is a software program that places your child in the role of a detective solving the slipper theft. Most children know who most likely stole Cinderella's slipper, but the real problem-solving task is to figure out logically what the detective should do while solving the crime. Problem-solving simulations, such as "Who Stole Cinderella's Slipper?", are quite engaging for they resemble a puzzle. As your child reads, he needs to think logically and develop sound reasons.

Simulation programs for personal computers are still in their infancy. Presently the memory capacity of personal computers limits the complexity of simulation programs. As computer technology progresses, simulations will become a great tool to develop advanced thinking and reading.

Another area of CAI is instructional games. As a parent, you're probably wary of computer games. And it's true—many computer games are of the "arcade" variety, with violence often the main focus to winning a game. But there are games available that do increase your child's learning and in a nonviolent manner. One such game is "Word Challenge," published by Proximity, which is similar to the popular game "Boggle." Your child is challenged to find more words than Lex, the computer, can. Lex presents a game board with scrambled letters next to each other. In three minutes, your child is to find words hidden in rows, columns, and diagonals (frontwards and backwards) as pictured below. At the end of three minutes, Lex identifies those words your child didn't find. What a motivating way to increase your child's word knowledge!

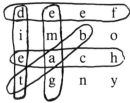

The last CAI category is demonstration. This program is exactly what it says. The program explains and shows how to do something. In the area of reading, a demonstration program may show a child how to read. Texas Instrument's software program "Magic Wand Books" demonstrates reading to preschoolers. A story is shown on the computer. The child uses a bar-code reader, which is somewhat similar to a light pen, to read the words on the page. To use this program, the computer requires an extra component known as a speech synthesizer. This component enables the computer to read the book aloud. Speech synthesizers aren't yet able to sound like a human voice and tend to be mechanical sounding. However, speech synthesizers will vastly improve in the next few years and will play a large role in teaching young children to read.

Word Processing

Word processing is not a CAI program nor a computer language, but it is an invaluable tool to help children learn to read and write. With word processing, typing is made easy. Corrections and additions are made simple. With a typewriter, if you want to place a new paragraph between the first and second paragraph on page two, you are forced to retype the page. But with a word processing program, inserting a paragraph is as easy as pressing a key. Easy computer commands allow your child to make all kinds of changes with speed and ease. Recently, a variety of word processing programs have been developed specifically for children. These programs can be quickly learned by most seven- and eight-year-olds.

A successful word processing program for children is the "Bank Street Writer," developed by teachers at Bank Street College. It is a popular program used by many elementary schools and can be purchased at local computer stores. Also, the "Bank Street Writer" will probably meet all family members' needs.

There is an extra bonus with word processing programs like the "Bank Street Writer." Your child will enjoy writing because many of those painful aggravating chores associated with writing are eliminated. Changes and corrections don't require retyping the entire project. Poor penmanship is no longer a problem. Rough drafts look like final drafts. Each draft is neat, since the computer eliminates such things as cross-outs, sentence reordering, and spelling errors. Included with some word processing programs is a dictionary that automatically corrects misspelled words. What an invaluable tool for writing!

You may wonder how word processing can increase your child's reading. Easy! Remember, when we first discussed in Chapter Two the Language Experience Approach in which your child dictated stories as you wrote them on paper? Now you have a computer to do this job! Your child can easily make changes but still have a perfect product at the end. No cross-outs are found in the original dictation, making it easier for him to read. You'll find your child will be willing to make more changes because his dictation always looks neat and attractive. And neat, perfect projects are very important to your preschoolers. Making changes and playing with language can only increase your child's ability to read and write. Now with the availability of word processing, your child's language growth can be easily increased.

The word processor is also a good tool for your seven-year-old or older youngster to use on his own. As your child writes, he is spending time rereading his writing. The more your child writes, the more he increases his reading power. Encourage your child to write using the computer. Show him how to make editorial changes and encourage him to do so. Print his stories and display them. The computer makes writing and reading enjoyable.

Leo and Olga Geoffrion have suggested a technique for using word processing to develop your child's vocabulary. Many words in our English language have multiple meanings. For example, the word "bay" has a variety of meanings. To teach your child about multiple meanings, use your word processor to compose a paragraph such as the one below.

> Joan's house is located on a beautiful *bay*. Her home is lovely with two beautiful *bay* windows. The outside of her house is painted in a rustic *bay* color which makes it quite attractive. There are many shrubs in Joan's front yard. She has hemlocks, *bay*,

yews, burning bushes, and many more. In her backyard, you can see Joan's beloved *bay* gracefully running around the fenced yard.

Ask your child to think of another word having the same meaning as the word "bay." Invite him to read the paragraph on the computer screen. Tell him to use the command "Replace." Now he can ask the computer to replace the word "bay" with his previously selected word. The paragraph now contains the selected word rather that the original word "bay." Reread the paragraph and discuss if the substituted word makes sense in each sentence. If not, why? Through discussion, lead him to realize that words often have multiple meanings, so in order to identify a word's meaning, he needs to read the sentence.

The nice feature of word processing is its instant capabilities to replace one word with another word and still not lose the original paragraph. Your child can keep substituting a new word for "bay" and check how each word affects the meaning of each sentence.

Your older child may find the word processor a good aid for taking and organizing notes. If your youngster is gathering information for a report, he'll find word processing will save him much time. For example, suppose his report topic is golden retrievers. He intends to write about the care, training, and breeding of golden retrievers. With a word processing program, he can set up files for each of these three areas. As he reads about an area, he can select a category, such as training, and type his notes. If he finds information on breeding, he can select the appropriate category and type in the information. When your child is ready to write his report, all information is contained in the appropriate category. Thus, report writing is less taxing than in the past when he relied on note cards, et cetera.

Specific software programs that contain note-taking systems are also available for report writing. Check with your local computer store to review these programs.

Computer as Mailman

In the past, communicating over telephone wires so a message could be instantaneously sent and an immediate response received required the capabilities of a large main frame computer system. Now personal computers have these same capabilities but at a lesser price.

Computer mail provides another opportunity to improve writing and reading skills. When your child needs information for a report, he can use his personal computer to electronically compose and mail his letter. Without too much delay, he receives his requested information. Can you remember doing reports and needing information? You sent a letter and hoped you'd receive an answer within a month. This is no longer a problem. Information is much more accessible and can be acquired at a much faster rate. When your child has to wait a month to receive information, enthusiasm and motivation are often lost. Computer mail overcomes such a problem.

Computer mail can be used for many different writing and reading activities, such as pen pals, thank-you notes, newspaper writing, and story writing. Reading and writing come alive with the use of a computer mail system. Additional purposeful and meaningful activities can be developed that increase your child's motivation and effort.

Software Programs: Which One?

Earlier in this chapter, I suggested that you become a critical consumer of software. If you have ever considered purchasing software, you know how expensive it is. Besides cost, you also want your child to be spending his time wisely. If the software doesn't motivate and increase learning, do you really want to purchase it? I have tried to be sensitive to these and other points as I prepared a list of standards for selecting reading software. If "yes" can be answered to a majority of the questions, the program's quality is above average. But, in the final analysis, you must be the judge.

1. Does the program provide good instruction in an area of reading (word recognition, vocabulary, comprehension, and study skills)?

2. Are the directions easy to understand, and can they be reviewed at any point in the program?

3. Is the content of the program of high quality?

4. Is the program logical and easy to follow?

5. Will the program challenge your child but is not so difficult that it discourages him?

6. Will the program actively involve your child in learning?

7. Does the program provide encouraging feedback so your child quickly knows if his responses are correct or incorrect?

8. Are there several levels of difficulty so that as your child advances, the program can also be increased in difficulty?

9. Can your child use the program again and again and still learn?

10. Will your child be interested in the program?

11. Are colorful graphics, animation, and sound effects used to keep your child's attention and still not detract from learning?

To answer these questions, you need to preview the program. You also may want your child to try the program before purchasing it. Some computer stores will set up a demonstration for you to use prior to purchase. If not, your local library may have a copy of the software program. If you are unable to preview the program, read the program manual. Many times there is sufficient information provided to answer the previous questions.

Another helpful resource for selecting software is computer magazines. Magazine reviews of software may be your only way to evaluate the program. They are quite helpful since experts are selected to review these programs

Unfortunately, there are still few quality reading software programs. Many lack creativity and challenge. Often they are too simple. In some software programs, the goal doesn't match the activity your child is doing while others teach insignificant reading skills or teach skills poorly. However, in all new technological advances, the first ones are usually somewhat crude and lack sophistication. As we approach the 90s, we'll see many advances in software programs. Such advances should improve the quality of software.

What Lies in the Future?

Geoffrion and Geoffrion suggest some exciting future uses of the computer for reading. Let's consider their futuristic outlooks.

Instead of looking up new words while reading a chapter in science, your child will be able to ask for a definition and, when necessary, seek further clarification. The computer will even use a picture to develop word meaning.

In the future, computers may present print in a different format. To make it easier for your child to understand the author's ideas, sentences may appear in logical units highlighting important words as we see in the illustration below. With the help of a computer, your child may be able to read more difficult books due to this automatic formating capability.

If it rains,
make sure you cover the electronic equipment.
If you see lightning,
make sure you head for the nearest marina.

If you have ever watched some of the commercials for new cars, you have probably seen the instant drawing of the new car appearing on the computer screen. Soon your child will read on the computer about the planning and designing of a wood deck and before his eyes the step-by-step building of the deck will occur. Can you imagine how much easier it will be for your child to apply what he has read?

Geoffrion and Geoffrion suggest that educational computers of the future will use more perfected speech synthesizers to help your child pronounce unknown words. With a touch on the screen or the use of a joystick, the computer voice will pronounce the word, give the definition, provide meaningful clues, or sound it out. The future may also include a computer that listens and corrects your child's oral reading errors.

In the future, computers will play a greater role in helping children read. Not only will schools have a computer for each child, but each family will have its own computer. Teachers and parents alike will be more involved in educating children. Greater cooperation between home and school will develop due, in part, to the promising future of computer technology.

Suggestions to Parents

1. You may be wondering which personal computer you should purchase. Many computer magazines compare and evaluate the personal computers on the market. When new hardware is developed, computer magazines often give reviews. Books on computers provide guidelines for selecting hardware. One such book is *Practical Guide to Computers in Education.* These and other sources can be invaluable in selecting the best personal computer for your family's needs.

2. To keep you and your child updated on the newest equipment and software programs, join a computer club. Talk to your local computer store for the names of clubs near your home. Computer clubs can provide a wealth of information and assistance.

3. Discuss with your child's teacher or your school's librarian software available for your computer. They can provide you with firsthand knowledge of which software programs are most beneficial for your child.

4. Use computer magazines to review reading software programs. *Personal Software* provides a monthly review of the best software available for your whole family. This magazine is available at newstands.

5. Your child may want to learn more about computers by reading the following books:

D'Ignazio, F. *The Star Wars Question and Answer Book About Computers.* New York: Random House, 1983.

D'Ignazio, F. *The Creative Kid's Guide to Home Computers.* New York: Doubleday, 1981.

Lampton, C. *Computer Languages.* New York: Franklin Watts, 1983.

Corbett, S. *Home Computers — A Simple and Informative Guide.* Boston, MA: Little, Brown, 1980.

For those who enjoy computers and reading fiction, try the following titles:

Levy, E. *The Computer That Said Steal Me.* New York: Four Winds, 1983.

D'Ignazio, F. *Katie and the Computer.* Morristown, NJ: Creative Computing, 1979.

Bromberg, A. *Computer Overbyte.* New York, Greenwillow, 1982.

6. If you're interested in acquiring more information about computers, let me suggest the next two books:

Coburn, P. et al. *Practical Guide to Computers in Education.* Reading, MA: Addison-Wesley, 1982.

Geoffrion, L.D. & Geoffrion, O.P. *Computers and Reading Instruction.* Reading, MA: Addison-Wesley, 1983.

7. Many public libraries extend borrowing privileges for computer software. This can provide your child with a greater variety of software and also can be a real money saver.

8. Many public libraries have access to computer data bases that locate magazines and books about a given topic. This service can easily help your junior high child with school reports or personal interests. Contact your local library for more specific information.

"IT'S OKAY FOR YOU TO SAY ARITHMETIC IS EASY. YOU FIGURE IN YOUR HEAD . . . I HAVE TO USE A COMPUTER!"

Chapter 10

PARENTS AND
TEACHERS AS PARTNERS

Schools are more effective when parents are an integral part of the system. The interest and participation parents provide can only benefit both child and teacher. Your support and cooperation can do wonders for your child's self-confidence and motivation as well as increase his learning. Teachers, too, appreciate the supportive parent. Your positive attitude will open doors to your child's classroom, and teachers will be more inclined to be honest and open about your child's strengths and weaknesses. Teachers tend to expend extra effort on teaching children when parents support and extend learning at home. An educational partnership can easily develop if both parent and teacher respect, trust, and cooperate with each other.

Parent-Teacher Conferences

Parent-teacher conferences are important in developing a successful school experience for your child. Let's consider specific guidelines to help you communicate effectively with your child's teacher. Practice these guidelines, and your child will reap the benefits.

- Guideline 1: *Identify the purpose for the conference.* Is it to become acquainted? Is it to alleviate your concerns about your child's poor attitude towards reading and/or school? Or is it to receive a report card and test scores? Each of these situations is vastly different and requires different preparation.

- Guideline 2: *Communicate the purpose for the conference.* If you are requesting the conference, immediately tell the teacher the purpose. This helps to alleviate any imagined fears the teacher may have about your request to hold a conference.

- Guideline 3: *Arrange the conference at the teacher's convenience.* The teacher then has sufficient time to plan and to have the necessary information at the conference. An unplanned conference can turn out to be a waste of time for both teacher and parent and cause feelings of frustration.

- Guideline 4: *Plan for the conference.* Write out the areas and questions you want the conference to cover. Combine, delete, and clarify these questions, and, finally, prioritize them. By using this process, your most important questions will be asked in a clear, succinct manner. Moreover, the teacher's responses will likely be clearer and more to the point.

- Guideline 5: *Restate the purpose of the conference at the onset.* Try to stay on the topic since your time together is limited.

- Guideline 6: *Display a positive attitude during the conference.* Be aware that not only what you say reflects your attitude, but also your tone of voice, facial expression, and body movements. A loud voice may imply dominance. Rigid posture may suggest anger or disapproval. Always listen attentively and show your enthusiasm.

- Guideline 7: *Remain open and supportive throughout the conference.* Don't become antagonistic or defensive; otherwise the conference outcome can be disastrous. Strive for cooperation between you and your child's teacher. Even when teachers present a negative side of your child's behavior or inform you of other problems, try to remain objective. This can be difficult when it is your child, but he will experience as many or more difficulties if you and the teacher don't try to find a way to work together to solve these problems.

- Guideline 8: *Make sure suggestions are provided to increase your child's achievement in reading and other areas.* Both school and home should be involved in the continual development of your child's growth. If your child is doing well, find out what you can do to ensure continued success and progress. If he has difficulties, make sure the teacher goes beyond merely pointing out a problem. The teacher needs to provide ideas for eliminating or reducing the difficulty. Many parents have been discouraged or aggravated because teachers point out problems but don't provide solutions. Don't let this situation occur! If immediate suggestions can't be provided, then a follow-up conference is needed.

- Guideline 9: *Ask for examples of daily work to better understand your child's strengths and weaknesses.* By reviewing your child's work, you will learn if progress has been made since the last conference. Have any weaknesses become more severe? If improvement hasn't been made, are other methods or materials being used? As a parent, what should you be doing at home with your child?

- Guideline 10: *Try not to become emotional during the conference.* Displaying anger, tears, etc.

during the conference does not help your child. You can show your emotions at another place and time. The conference time is valuable and should be used to develop solutions.

- Guideline 11: *Clarify and summarize each important point as it is discussed.* Thus, both teacher and parent are better able to develop a mutual understanding and agreement. Let's look at a conference in which a parent does a good job of clarifying and summarizing a major point.

Teacher: Susan has difficulties with oral reading. She is not reading smoothly and tends to read in a word-by-word fashion. If Susan reads along with a taped version of a book, her oral reading would improve. Can you provide Susan with taped versions of books?

Parent: Susan is a poor reader. Do you want me to make tapes of books so Susan can read along with the tape?

Teacher: Yes, you can make tapes, but the public and school library can also provide you with tapes and books. Also, I would like to clarify one point about Susan's reading ability. She has some difficulty with oral reading, but I would not classify her as a poor reader.

Parent: Thank-you for the clarification. Susan and I will work together on improving oral reading. We will check the school and the public library for some books and tapes.

If the parent hadn't summarized and clarified what was heard in this conference, a misconception might have developed. By suggesting that she would tape books for Susan, the parent was able to find out if the suggestion was appropriate as well as learning about alternatives. Notice that this parent summarized the conference at the end so both parties received the same message.

229

- Guideline 12: *Once agreement is reached, discuss the next topic.* During the conference, you may want the teacher to understand certain things about your child. Or you may have a specific request. Once your point is understood and the teacher has agreed, it is wise not to continue the same discussion. It may present new questions which may reverse the previously made agreement. Once a decision is made, it is best to start discussing the next point. You will find the conference to be much more productive.

- Guideline 13: *Make sure you understand the information the teacher is supplying.* Often teachers use educational jargon, not realizing parents don't understand. Don't be afraid to ask for an explanation or definition. Make sure when the conference ends you have understood all the information reported. If you're confused or uncertain, your child won't benefit and learning may be hindered.

- Guideline 14: *Keep conferences short.* Conferences that run more than 40 minutes can be tiresome for both parent and teacher. If you can't accomplish all that has been planned, ask for another conference. By scheduling a future conference, you will have an opportunity to follow up on previous agreements and revise them if necessary.

What Should Parents Learn from Conferences?

The purpose of a conference is to communicate information. In most cases, the information to be communicated concerns your child's progress in school. At such conferences, grades should be explained. You should understand how these grades have been reached. Are grades determined by comparing your child to others in the class? Or is he compared to his own abilities? Strengths and weaknesses should also be pinpointed, and examples of your child's work should be used to illustrate these areas. Tapes of your child's oral reading from the beginning and the end of the year can demonstrate progress or lack of progress better than a teacher's verbal explanation. Dated samples of daily work is another way to illustrate your child's typical strengths and weaknesses. Checklists of acquired reading skills can be helpful at conferences if teachers explain the checklist thoroughly.

At the conclusion of the conference, you should feel that you have gained some valuable information about your child's abilities, about his strengths and weaknesses, and how you can help overcome these weaknesses. If you need additional information, make sure you schedule another conference in the near future.

What is Going on in School?

Some conferences should provide information about your child's scholastic ability but you also need information about the school program to gain insight into your child's progress and ability as well as opportunities to increase his skills. Information about the school program can be gleaned from individual conferences with your child's teacher, principal, or curriculum director. This information can also be provided at open houses, parent-teacher meetings, or grade-level meetings. Use the following questions during these kinds of conferences to help you learn about the school reading and other programs.

1. What specific areas of reading instruction (word recognition, vocabulary, comprehension, study skills, and recreational reading) receive the most emphasis? Are certain areas of reading given more emphasis at different grade levels? If so, what are the areas for each grade level?

2. Are special programs available such as remedial reading, learning disabilities, speech therapy, gifted reading, et cetera? If so, how is a child referred to such programs?

3. What is the policy on homework at each grade level?

4. How are children generally grouped for instruction? Is there a specific way of grouping children for instruction?

5. How are children evaluated? Are they compared to their own abilities or compared to those at their grade level?

6. What major skills or projects are required at each grade level?

7. Are there a variety of methods used to teach reading?

There is not just a single, acceptable response for each of the above questions, but the following guidelines can be used to evaluate school professionals' replies.

In general, the instructional emphasis at all grade levels should be comprehension—understanding and applying what is learned from print. Another emphasis should be to create lifelong readers. Instruction should motivate children to read. During the primary grades (1-3), many schools heavily stress word recognition skills, such as phonics, sight words, dictionary, et cetera. Word recognition is important but shouldn't overshadow the importance of comprehension. If too much instructional time is focused on word recognition, then the result may often be a child who doesn't understand the purpose for reading and doesn't enjoy it. Moreover, when interest is squelched, teachers and parents often experience difficulty in developing or renewing a child's love of reading.

To the second question on special programs, an affirmative response should be made. Each school should be concerned with helping children reach their potential. Thus, what is needed are specific programs for those children with special needs. Otherwise, our children are being deprived. Not only are special programs necessary, but they also need to be staffed by professionals who are specifically trained to work with children exhibiting special needs. A program is only as good as its personnel.

There are many different views on homework. Some believe children are in school for six to seven hours a day and need time after school to develop other areas. Others argue that children need further practice beyond the school day. I believe that homework is sometimes necessary but I prefer that, whenever possible, the child has free time to read books of his choice. Children who read for leisure are practicing and increasing their reading skills as well as expanding their knowledge of language and general information. Recreational reading is high on my priority list and should receive adequate attention. It is also an easy activity for parent involvement. No elaborate materials are necessary, only a good book, magazine or newspaper. Sharing what is read is a natural outgrowth of recreational reading when child and parents read every day for enjoyment.

Grouping for instruction is another issue in which educators don't always agree. There is as much research indicating that one type of grouping is superior to another as there is indicating the opposite to be true. It is important, however, that each child be a member of several different groups. At times, your child should be working with children at his ability level, but at other times he needs to be challenged by those who have greater abilities. In the same manner, your child needs to be the one to stimulate thinking of those with less ability. All these experiences encourage the total development of a child. Your child also needs the opportunity to work in large groups, small groups, and individual activities. Such experiences enhance learning. Any single grouping pattern or group size, used to the exclusion of others, can be detrimental to your child's learning.

The fifth question about student evaluation has always been a "touchy" issue. Should a child be compared to others in his age group or be compared to his own abilities? There exists as many pros as cons to these two questions. The greatest concern is the child's self-concept. If the evaluation system has negative effects on the child's self-esteem, then motivation and interest will be harmed.

When this occurs, it becomes increasingly difficult to stimulate a child to overcome his weaknesses. Young children with low abilities who are compared to their peers may experience real defeat. We should encourage young children rather than discourage them from learning.

Knowing the major skills and projects required at specific grade levels can benefit your child. You can help your child learn these skills and prepare him for major projects. Work with your child's teacher to reinforce skills and develop quality projects.

Hopefully, your child's teachers are using a variety of reading methods and materials to teach reading. As discussed in Chapter Three, no one method has been shown to be superior to another. Each method, (language experience, basal, phonics, and individualized) has strengths and weaknesses. A good teacher uses the best parts of each to teach your child to read.

Cementing Your Relationship

Conferences should not be the only time you and your child's teacher meet. Both parent and teacher need to be involved in other school functions. Often, both parents are employed and can't be involved in morning and afternoon activities, such as volunteer tutors, room mothers or fathers, library assistants, et cetera. However, these roles do further your relationship with your child's teacher and can be rewarding. But these aren't the only ways you can become involved.

Think for a moment about your present participation in your child's school. Are you a member of the local parent-teacher organization? If so, do you attend meetings regularly? Are you serving on the organization's board? Do you participate in their planned functions? Parent-teacher organizations provide another opportunity to become acquainted with your child's teacher and can foster better communication between school and home.

Do you attend school board meetings? Are you

knowledgeable about the school board's educational plans? Are you actively supporting the needs of your child's teachers? To show your support, have you communicated with individual board members or spoken at a board meeting? Board decisions often affect the quality of your child's education. Be well informed and participate! You may want to serve as a school board member. What better way can you become involved?

Have you offered your time for special classroom activities, such as science fairs, plays, or other school programs? Have you volunteered to speak to your child's class about your career or hobbies? Teachers need knowledgeable speakers to discuss topics studied at school. And an extra pair of hands is always needed at special events. One-time activities allow working parents to be involved in their child's school experience. They also provide parents with another opportunity to become better acquainted with their child's teacher.

There are additional ways to enhance your relationship with your child's teacher. Have you followed through on mutually agreed upon suggestions to help your child learn? This is important to establish an open and trusting relationship. If you don't follow through, the teacher may question your commitment. Or the teacher may wonder if you really agreed with her suggestion or didn't want her help or advice. Either situation diminishes communication and trust.

Last, but not least, it is important to show your appreciation to excellent teachers. A note of praise and thanks is welcomed by any teacher. It is also thoughtful to send a letter to the principal, superintendent, or school board commending this teacher's outstanding ability and commitment.

Try to think of additional ways to further your relationship with your child's teacher. A strong parent-teacher partnership will enhance a child's school performance.

Some Final Thoughts

As a parent, you are capable of teaching your child to achieve in school. Parents who take an active role can help to increase their child's motivation, interest, and achievement. Your child will be a good student if parents and teachers work together. As you help your child develop into a competent student, try to apply the following principles.

1. Read to your child and have him read to you.
2. Surround your child with a wide variety of books, magazines, and newspapers. Encourage him to read fiction, poetry, folk tales, biographies, et cetera.
3. Read yourself and establish a time every day for leisurely family reading. Your child can only learn to read by reading.
4. Emphasize that the purpose of reading is to comprehend. Suggest he always develop a purpose or question before he reads.
5. Take your child to the library and encourage him to select books that interest him. Share these books. Discuss what he has learned and ask him questions beyond the factual level.
6. Relate new learning to old and familiar ideas so your child can easily understand and learn new information.
7. Encourage your child to talk about things he has learned. Provide him with additional ideas and vocabulary to further his knowledge.
8. Provide your child with background information before he reads. The information increases understanding and enjoyment.
9. Explore together our great big wondrous world and discuss what you have seen and learned.

10. Do not push your child to succeed but encourage and support him in his learning.

11. Expect that your child will make mistakes no matter what his abilities may be. Encourage him to take risks in learning and make mistakes because this is the way to learn and increase knowledge.

12. Praise your child for his accomplishments. Everyone wants to be noticed when they are succeeding.

13. Be proud of your child no matter what his ability may be. The learning disabled as well as the gifted need parental pride and support.

14. Be interested in your child's learning. Join the local parent-teacher organization and become actively involved.

15. Participate in your child's learning. Talk to your child's teacher and become an active partner in teaching and learning.

By following these principles and carrying through the activities described in the foregoing chapters, your child will not only be interested in reading, but will develop into a youngster who achieves success in all academic areas.

REFERENCES

RECOMMENDED
CHILDREN'S LITERATURE

Picture Books

Adams, P. & Jones, C. *I Thought I Saw.* Restrop Manor, England: Child's Play, 1974.

Adler, D.A. *Bunny Rabbit Rebus.* New York: Crowell, 1983.

Alexander, M. *Nobody Asked Me If I Wanted a Baby Sister.* New York: Dial, 1971.

Alexander, M. *Sabrina.* New York: Dial, 1971.

Anderson, H.C. *Thumbelina.* New York: Dial, 1979.

Anderson, H.C. *The Little Match Girl.* Boston: Houghton Mifflin, 1968.

Bate, L. *Little Rabbit's Loose Tooth.* New York: Crown, 1975.

Bemelmans, L. *Madeline.* New York: Viking, 1939.

Burningham, J. *The School.* New York: Crowell, 1975.

Carle, E. *The Very Hungry Caterpillar.* New York: World, 1969.

Daugherty, J. *Andy and the Lion.* New York: Viking, 1966.

de Paola, T. *Strega Nona.* Englewood Cliffs, NJ: Prentice-Hall, 1975.

Dobrin, A. *Scat.* New York: Four Winds, 1971.

Duvoisin, R. *Petunia.* New York: Alfred A. Knopf, 1950.

Estes, E. *A Little Oven.* New York: Harcourt, Brace & World, 1955.

Gag, W. *Millions of Cats.* New York: Coward-McCann, 1928.

Hoban, R. *Bedtime For Francis.* New York: Harper & Row, 1960.

Hutchins. *Rosie's Walk.* New York: Macmillan, 1968.

Hutchins, P. *Titch.* New York: Macmillan, 1971.

Johnson, C. *Harold and the Purple Crayon.* New York: Harper Row, 1955.

Keats, E.J. *Peter's Chair.* New York: Harper Row, 1967.

Krauss, R. *The Carrot Seed.* New York: Harper Row, 1945.

Lionni, L. *Swimmy.* New York: Pantheon, 1963.

Lobel, A. *Fables.* New York: Harper Row, 1980.

Lobel, A. *Frog and Toad Are Friends.* New York: Harper Row, 1970.

McCloskey, R. *Make Way for Ducklings.* New York: Viking, 1941.

McCloskey, R. *Lentil.* New York: Viking, 1940.

McGovern, A. *Too Much Noise.* Boston: Houghton Mifflin, 1967.

McPhail, D. *The Bear's Toothache.* Boston: Little Brown, 1972.

Ormondroyd, E. *Theodore.* Berkeley, CA: Parnassus, 1966.

Potter, B. *The Tale of Peter Rabbit.* New York: Warne, 1958.

Rey, H.A. *Curious George.* Boston: Houghton Mifflin, 1941.

Sendak, M. *Where the Wild Things Are.* New York: Harper Row, 1963.

Seuss, Dr. *Horton Hatches the Egg.* New York: Random House, 1940.

Steig, W. *Caleb & Kate.* New York: Farrar, Straus, & Giroux, 1977.

Tolstoy, A. *The Great Big Enormous Turnip.* New York: Watts, 1968.

Turlaynewberry, C. *Marshmallow.* New York: Harper & Brothers, 1942.

Viorst, J. *Alexander and the Terrible, Horrible, No Good, Very Bad Day!* New York: Atheneum, 1972.

Waber, B. *Ira Sleeps Over.* Boston: Houghton Mifflin, 1972.

Wahl, J. *The Muffletumps.* New York: Holt, Rinehart, & Winston, 1966.

Wildsmith, B. *Pelican.* New York: Pantheon, 1982.

Williams, M. *The Velveteen Rabbit.* Garden City, New York: Doubleday, 1926.

Winslow, M. *Mud Pies and Other Recipes.* New York: Macmillan, 1961.

Wright, D. *Edith & Mr. Bear.* New York: Random House, 1964.

Zion, G. *Harry the Dirty Dog.* New York: Harper Row, 1978.

Zolotow, C. *My Grandson.* New York: Harper Row, 1971.

Very Easy-to-Read Picture Books

Berenstain, S. & Berenstain, J. *The Berenstain Bears and the Spooky Old Tree.* New York: Beginner, 1978.

Breinburg, P. *Shawn Goes to School.* New York: Crowell, 1973.

Brown, M.W. *Where Have You Been?* New York: Hastings House, 1981.

Brown, M.W. *Goodnight Moon.* New York: Harper & Row, 1977.

Bruna, D. *I Can Read.* New York: Methuen, 1965.

Burningham, J. *The Dog.* New York: Crowell, 1976.

Charles, D. *Calico Cat's Exercise Book.* Chicago: Children's Press, 1982.

DeCaprio, A. *The Bus From Chicago.* New York: Wonder, 1965.

Hamsa, B. *Dirty Larry.* Chicago: Children's Press, 1983.

Hill, E. *Spot's Birthday Party.* New York: G.P. Putnam's Sons, 1982.

Johnson, C. *A Picture for Harold's Room.* New York: Harper & Row, 1960.

Krauss, R. *The Birthday Party.* New York: Harper & Row, 1957.

Lenski, L. *I Like Winter.* New York: Henry Walck, 1950.

Mayer, M. *If I Had . . .* New York: Dial, 1968.

Matthais, C. *Over-Under.* Chicago: Children's Press, 1984.

Moncure, J.B. *Hide-And-Seek Word Bird.* Elgin, IL: Child's World, 1982.

Paterson, D. *Eat!* New York: Dial, 1975.

Wordless Picture Books

de Paola, T. *Pancakes for Breakfast.* New York: Harcourt, Brace, Jovanovich, 1978.

Goodall, J.S. *An Edwardian Christmas.* New York: Atheneum, 1978.

Krahn, F. *Robot-Bot-Bot.* New York: E.P. Dutton, 1979.

Krahn, F. *Sebastian and the Mushroom.* New York: Delacorte, 1976.

Mayer, M. *Frog, Where Are You?* New York: Dial, 1969.

Shaw, C. *It Looked Like Spilt Milk.* New York: Harper Row, 1947.

Turkle, B. *Deep in the Forest.* New York: E.P. Dutton, 1976.

Winten, P. *The Bear and the Fly*. New York: Crown, 1976.

Easy-to-Read Nonfiction Series

A New True Book. Chicago: Children's Press.
This is a series of easy-to-read science and social studies books. Some of the books in the series are:

Computers	*Airports*
Newspapers	*Ships and Seaports*
Money	*Volcanoes*
Conservation	*Weather Experiments*
United Nations	

Lerner Publications from Minneapolis, Minnesota, have published a series of sports books. Some of the titles are:

Sailing Is for Me
Canoeing Is for Me
Synchronized Swimming Is for Me
Soccer Is for Me

Books for Young Explorers. National Geographic Society
This is a series of easy-to-read science books. Included are beautiful detailed photographs. Some of the books in the series are:

Life in Ponds and Streams
How Animals Hide
Zoo Babies
Creatures Small and Furry

Fiction — Grades 3 to 5

Bond, M. *A Bear Called Paddington*. Boston: Houghton Mifflin, 1958.

Brink, C.R. *Caddie Woodlawn*. New York: Macmillan, 1970.

Brittain, B. *The Wish Giver*. New York: Harper Row, 1983.

Cleary, B. *The Mouse and the Motorcycle*. New York: Morrow, 1965.

Cleary, B. *Henry Huggins*. New York: Morrow, 1950.

Dahl, R. *James and the Giant Peach*. New York: Knopf, 1961.

Danziger, P. *The Cat Ate My Gymsuit*. New York: Delacorte, 1974.

DeJong, M. *The Wheel on the School*. New York: Harper Row, 1955.

Eager, E. *Half Magic*. New York: Harcourt, Brace, Jovanovich, 1954.

Edmonds, W. *The Matchlock Gun*. New York: Dodd, Mead, 1942.

Grahame, K. *Mole's Christmas*. Englewood Cliffs, NJ: Prentice-Hall, 1982.

Haywood, C. *B is for Betsy*. New York: Harcourt, Brace, & World, 1967.

Henry, M. *King of the Wind*. Chicago: Rand McNally, 1948.

Hildick, E.W. *The Case of the Slingshot Sniper*. New York: Macmillan, 1983.

Lewis, C.S. *The Lion, The Witch, and The Wardrobe*. New York: Macmillan, 1950.

Lindgren, A. *Pippi Longstocking*. New York: Viking, 1950.

McCloskey, R. *Homer Price*. New York: Viking, 1943.

North, S. *Rascal*. New York: Dutton, 1963.

Norton, M. *The Borrowers*. New York: Harcourt, Brace, Jovanovich, 1953.

Patterson, K. *Bridge to Terabithia*. New York: Avon, 1980.

Robertson, K. *Henry Reed, Inc*. New York: Viking, 1958.

Rockwell, T. *How to Eat Fried Worms*. New York: Watts, 1973.

Selden, G. *The Cricket in Times Square*. New York: Farrar, Straus, & Giroux, 1960.

Sobel, D.J. Encyclopedia Brown, Boy Detective. New York: Scholastic, 1963.

White, E.B. *Charlotte's Web*. New York: Harper Row, 1952.

Wilder, L.I. *Little House in the Big Woods*. New York: Harper Row, 1932.

Williams, J. & Abrashkin, R. *Danny Dunn and the Homework Machine*. New York: McGraw-Hill, 1958.

Fiction — Grades 6 to 8

Aiken, J. *The Wolves of Willoughby Chase*. Garden City, NJ: Doubleday, 1963.

Alexander, L. *The Castle of Llyr*. New York: Holt, Rinehart, & Winston, 1966.

Avallone, M. *5-Minute Mysteries*. New York: Scholastic, 1968.

Babbitt, N. *Tuck Everlasting*. New York: Farrar, Straus, & Giroux, 1975.

Bell, C. *Ratha's Creature*. New York: Atheneum, 1983.

Blume, J. *Are You There God? It's Me Margaret*. Scarsdale, NY: Bradbury, 1970.

Bond, N. *A Place to Come Back To*. New York: Atheneum, 1984.

Byars, B. *Summer of the Swans*. New York: Viking, 1970.

Cormier, R. *I Am the Cheese*. New York: Pantheon, 1977.

Craighead, J. *Julie of the Wolves*. New York: Harper Row, 1972.

George, J. *My Side of the Mountain*. New York: Dutton, 1959.

Greene, B. *Summer of My German Soldier*. New York: Dial, 1973.

Guest, J. *Ordinary People*. New York: Viking, 1976.

Hinton, S.E. *Outsiders*. New York: Viking, 1967.

Kerr, J. *The Other Way Around*. New York: Coward, McCann, & Geoghegan, 1975.

Kerr, J. *When Hitler Stole Pink Rabbit*. New York: Coward, McCann, & Geoghegan, 1972.

Kerr, M.E. *Gentlehands*. New York: Harper Row, 1978.

Klein, N. *Mom, the Wolf Man, and Me*. New York: Pantheon, 1972.

Konigsburg, E.L. *From the Mixed-Up Files of Mrs. Basil E. Frankweiler*. New York: Atheneum, 1967.

Mark, J. *Thunder and Lightning*. New York: Crowell, 1967.

Neufield, J. *Edgar Allen*. New York: Phillips, 1968.

Patterson, K. *Jacob Have I Loved*. New York: Harper Row, 1980.

Raskin, E. *The Westing Game*. New York: Dutton, 1978.

Rawls, W. *Where the Red Fern Grows*. Garden City, NY: Doubleday, 1961.

Snyder, Z.K. *The Egypt Game*. New York: Atheneum, 1970.

Wells, H.G. *The Time Machine*. New York: Bantam, 1968.

Zindel, P. *The Pigman*. New York: Harper Row, 1968.

Zindel, P. & Zindel, B. *A Star for the Latecomer*. New York: Bantam, 1981.

REGULAR PHONIC ELEMENTS

Consonants: b, c, d, f, g, h, j, k, l, m, n, p, q, r, s, t, v, w, x, y, z

Consonant Clusters

Consonant Blends: bl, br, cl, cr, dr, fl, fr, gl, gr, pl, pr, sc, sk, sl, sm, sn, sp, st, sw, scr, str, tr, tw

Consonant Digraphs: ch, gh, ng, ph, sh, th

Word Families:

_ab	_ast	_ead	_id	_ob	_ub
_ace	_at	_eak	_ide	_ock	_ube
_ack	_ate	_ear	_ife	_oil	_uck
_ad	_aw	_eat	_ig	_ook	_uff
_ag	_ax	_ed	_ike	_ool	_ug
_aid	_ay	_eed	_ilt	_oom	_ull
_aim		_eep	_im	_op	_um
_air		_ell	_in	_orn	_un
_ake		_end	_ind	_ot	_unk
_all		_et	_ink	_ow	_ut
_am			_ip	_ox	
_amp			_it	_oy	
_an			_ite		
_and			_ix		
_ank					
_ap					
_ard					
_ark					

cv̆c	cv̄cé	**r-controlled vowels**
a	*a*	*a*
cab	cage	car
bad	rake	mark
rag	tame	tart
ham	tape	
ran	lace	
cap	mate	
rat	save	
e	*e*	*e*
red	-o-	-o-
den		
bet		
i	*i*	*i*
fin	ride	fir
hip	bike	
kit	mile	
mix	time	
	kite	
	mice	
o	*o*	*o*
job	code	bore
hop	joke	corn
cot	cope	
u	*u*	*u*
cub	cube	turn
bug	mute	
hum		
fun		

SCIENCE ROOTS

anthro   ⟶   anthropology
aster   ⟶   astronomy
bio   ⟶   biology
chron   ⟶   chronometer
derma   ⟶   dermatology
gene   ⟶   genetics
geo   ⟶   geology
hemo   ⟶   hemoglobin
hydr   ⟶   hydrochloride
meter   ⟶   barometer
logy   ⟶   psychology
photo   ⟶   photosynthesis
scope   ⟶   microscope
tele   ⟶   telegraph
terr   ⟶   territory
therm   ⟶   thermometer

HIGH FREQUENCY SIGHT WORDS

Revised Dolch List
Jerry L. Johns
Northern Illinois University

a	don't	in	only	think
about	down	into	open	this
across	draw	is	or	those
after	eat	it	other	thought
again	enough	its	our	three
all	even	just	out	through
always	every	keep	over	to
am	far	kind	own	today
an	fast	know	play	together
and	find	last	put	told
another	first	leave	ran	too
any	five	left	read	took
are	for	let	red	toward
around	found	light	right	try
as	four	like	round	turn
ask	from	little	run	two
at	full	long	said	under
away	gave	look	same	up
be	get	made	saw	upon
because	give	make	say	us
been	go	many	see	use
before	going	may	she	very
began	gone	me	short	walk
best	good	mean	should	want
better	got	might	show	warm
big	green	more	six	was
black	grow	most	small	we

blue	had	much	so	well
both	hard	must	some	went
bring	has	my	soon	were
but	have	near	start	what
by	he	need	still	when
call	heard	never	stop	where
came	help	next	take	which
can	her	new	tell	while
close	here	no	ten	white
cold	high	not	than	who
come	him	now	that	why
could	his	of	the	will
cut	hold	off	their	with
did	hot	oh	them	work
didn't	how	old	then	would
do	I	on	there	yes
does	I'm	once	these	yet
done	if	one	they	you
				your